WJEC EDUQAS GCSE | Work

English Language Practice Papers

Natalie Simpson
Julie Swain

OXFORD
UNIVERSITY PRESS

Great Clarendon Street, Oxford, OX2 6DP, United Kingdom

Oxford University Press is a department of the University of Oxford.

It furthers the University's objective of excellence in research, scholarship, and education by publishing worldwide. Oxford is a registered trade mark of Oxford University Press in the UK and in certain other countries

© Oxford University Press 2020

The moral rights of the authors have been asserted.

First published in 2020

All rights reserved. No part of this publication may be reproduced, stored in a retrieval system, or transmitted, in any form or by any means, without the prior permission in writing of Oxford University Press, or as expressly permitted by law, by licence or under terms agreed with the appropriate reprographics rights organization. Enquiries concerning reproduction outside the scope of the above should be sent to the Rights Department, Oxford University Press, at the address above.

You must not circulate this work in any other form and you must impose this same condition on any acquirer

British Library Cataloguing in Publication Data

Data available

ISBN 978-138-201432-8

10 9 8 7 6 5 4 3 2 1

Paper used in the production of this book is a natural, recyclable product made from wood grown in sustainable forests.

The manufacturing process conforms to the environmental regulations of the country of origin.

Printed in Great Britain by Bell and Bain Ltd., Glasgow

Acknowledgements
The authors and publisher are grateful for permission to include extracts from the following copyright material:

Max Campbell: 'Sailing Solo Across the Atlantic', *Yachting World*, May 2019, copyright © TI Media Ltd 2019, www.yachtingworld.com, used by permission of TI Media Ltd.

Leah Davis: 'Camden Market: My Favorite Day Out in London' from *The Sweetest Way* travel blog (2016), copyright © Leah Davis 2016, 2020, used by permission of the author.

Ken Follett: *Night Over Water* (Macmillan, 2019), copyright © Ken Follett 1991, used by permission of Pan Macmillan through PLSclear.

Penelope Lively: 'The Slovenian Giantess' from *Beyond the Blue Mountain* (Penguin, 1998), copyright © Penelope Lively 1998, used by permission of David Higham Associates Ltd on behalf of the author.

The publisher and authors would like to thank the following for permission to use photographs and other copyright material:

Cover: Gordon Scammell/Alamy Stock Photo

Contents

Introduction	4
WJEC Eduqas GCSE English Language specification overview	4
How this workbook is structured	5
What are the main features within this workbook?	5

Chapter 1: Component 1	
Component 1 sample exam paper	6
Preparing to practise	10
Section A	10
Section B	15
Understanding the mark scheme	16
Section A	16
Section B	32

Chapter 2: Component 1	
Component 1 sample exam paper	38
Preparing to practise	42
Section A	42
Section B	47
Understanding the mark scheme	48
Section A	48
Section B	64
Component 1: Progress check	70

Chapter 3: Component 2	
Component 2 sample exam paper	72
Preparing to practise	76
Section A	76
Section B	82
Understanding the mark scheme	84
Section A	84
Section B	102

Chapter 4: Component 2	
Component 2 sample exam paper	108
Preparing to practise	112
Section A	112
Section B	118
Understanding the mark scheme	120
Section A	120
Section B	137
Component 2: Progress check	142

Key terms glossary	144

Introduction

WJEC Eduqas GCSE English Language specification overview

The grade you receive at the end of your WJEC Eduqas GCSE English Language course is entirely based on your performance in two exam papers. The following provides a summary of how you will be assessed.

Exam paper	Questions and marks	Assessment Objectives

Component 1: 20th-century Literature Reading Study and Creative Prose Writing (40% of GCSE)	**Section A: Reading**
	 Exam text:
	 • One unseen extract from a 20th-century literary fiction text (approx. 60–100 lines)
	 Exam questions and marks:
	 • Five reading questions (40 marks), consisting of:
	   o Two short form question (2 x 5 marks)
	   o Three long form questions (3 x 10 marks)
		• AO1
		 • AO2
		 • AO4

	Section B: Writing Narrative writing task Exam question and marks: • One extended writing question (out of a choice of 4) • 40 marks (24 marks for Content and Organisation, 16 marks for Technical Accuracy)	• AO5 • AO6

Component 2: 19th- and 21st-century Non-fiction Reading Study and Transactional/Persuasive Writing (60% of GCSE)	**Section A: Reading**
	 Exam texts:
	 • One unseen extract from a 19th-century non-fiction text
	 • One unseen extract from a 21st-century non-fiction text
	 Exam questions and marks:
	 • Six reading questions (40 marks), consisting of:
	   o Three short form questions (2 x 3 marks and 1 x 4 marks)
	   o Three long form questions (3 x 10 marks)
		• AO1
		 • AO2
		 • AO3
		 • AO4

	Section B: Writing Transactional, persuasive and/or discursive writing task Exam question and marks: • Two extended writing tasks • 20 marks each (12 marks for Content and Organisation, 8 marks for Technical Accuracy for each task)	• AO5 • AO6

Assessment Objectives	
AO1	• Identify and interpret explicit and implicit information and ideas. • Select and synthesise evidence from different texts.
AO2	Explain, comment on and analyse how writers use language and structure to achieve effects and influence readers, using relevant subject terminology to support their views.
AO3	Compare writers' ideas and perspectives, as well as how these are conveyed, across two or more texts.
AO4	Evaluate texts critically and support this with appropriate textual references.
AO5	• Communicate clearly, effectively and imaginatively, selecting and adapting tone, style and register for different forms, purposes and audiences. • Organise information and ideas, using structural and grammatical features to support coherence and cohesion of texts.
AO6	Use a range of vocabulary and sentence structures for clarity, purpose and effect, with accurate spelling and punctuation.

Introduction

How this workbook is structured

The workbook is divided into four chapters. The chapters are self-contained so they can be used in any order.

- Chapter 1 and Chapter 2 focus on Component 1. Each chapter consists of a complete stand-alone exam paper: source texts, question paper and mark scheme. The source texts reflect the type of text you will be reading and responding to in your exam and the questions are also typical of what you will encounter. There are then follow-up sections with advice and activities so that you can improve the quality of your initial responses after you have attempted each practice Component 1 exam paper.

- Chapter 3 and Chapter 4 focus on Component 2. Again, each chapter consists of a complete stand-alone exam paper: source texts, question paper and mark scheme. The source texts reflect the type of texts you will be reading and responding to in your exam and the questions are also typical of what you will encounter. Again, there are then follow-up sections with advice and activities so that you can improve the quality of your initial responses after you have attempted each practice Component 2 exam paper.

What are the main features within this workbook?

Preparing to practise

Before you attempt each practice exam paper, you are reminded of which skills are being assessed in each question and what you are expected to do to demonstrate those skills.

Understanding the mark scheme

Before you attempt each practice exam paper, the mark scheme is unpicked to show how marks are awarded by the examiner. Key words in the mark scheme are explained and sample student answers at different levels are provided. This can help you to improve the quality of your work because you will understand exactly what is expected of you in each question.

Activities

After you have attempted the practice exam paper, you will find activities to help you improve your initial responses for each question.

> **Activity**

Tips

You will find tips on how best to approach each question in the exam paper.

> **Tip**

Upgrade

There are also tips to help you move up the mark scheme and focus on specific areas to improve.

> **Upgrade**

Key terms

This feature helps support your understanding of key terms. For ease of reference, there is also a complete list of key terms at the end of the workbook.

> **Key term**

Progress check

At the end of Chapter 2 and Chapter 4 you will find Progress checks. These enable you to use self-assessment to establish how confident you feel about what you have been learning for each Component and help you to identify areas for further practice.

> **Progress check**

5

Chapter 1: Component 1

Component 1 sample exam paper

This story is about an English woman called Eleanor who has been attending a conference in Europe.

Eva was a lecturer at the University of Zagreb and Eleanor was not sure that she liked her that much. Around forty, a few years older than herself, Eva was a somewhat frenzied woman with a mane of wiry black hair. […] She had battened on to Eleanor throughout the three days of the conference. This expedition to the lake on the final afternoon was at her insistence. The concluding sessions left Eleanor with four hours to spare before check-in time for her flight back to London. When Eva discovered this she had proposed a trip to the mountain lake. 'You will have your luggage with you and then I take you straight to the airport.'

Eleanor had demurred, partly on account of a certain lack of enthusiasm for Eva's company, but also because it was clear that a longish drive would be involved. By that time the countdown to departure would have begun and the airport would be exercising its magnetic pull. She had not much faith in Eva's time sense, or indeed in her battered little car. She had made excuses, but Eva would have none of it. 'You don't trust me, Eleanor. You think I will not get you to your plane.' And so decency had required a gracious acceptance and now here they were. […] Never mind, thought Eleanor, never mind. All part of life's rich pattern. By 6:30 I'll be on BA354 to Heathrow. Home by eleven, with any luck. […]

'We will drive to the hotel for lunch. And we will talk about where I can apply for a study grant in England next year,' [said Eva].

Yes, thought Eleanor, I suppose that is what we're here for, if the truth were told. No, that's a disgraceful thought. She is merely being hospitable to a visitor.

'This hotel is built quite recently,' said Eva. 'It is all newly laid out. They are hoping to attract foreign tourists and conferences.'

The entire lakeside resort had a doleful air of incompletion and abandonment. The pedestrian shopping precinct was a miniature townscape of empty windows and unpeopled walkways. The skating-rink and putting-green were closed. There was hardly anyone around. Eva led Eleanor into the hotel, which was equally deserted. They made their way through vast lounges in which oversized sofas and chairs bleakly confronted one another, and thence into a dining-room, one wall of which was a great sheet of glass overlooking the lake. Waiters wearing tuxedos converged upon them, proffering wine lists and urging them to make their selection from the cold buffet at the other side of the room.

Surveying this spread, Eleanor was again seized with a sense of the surreal. Whole salmon garnished with skewered twists of cucumber and lemon. Other cold fish, piped with rosettes of mayonnaise. Ranks of different kinds of salad, platters of sliced meats. Little bowls of caviar on ice.

'All for us?'

'Perhaps they are expecting some conference,' said Eva. […]

They returned to their table with heaped plates. The weather had improved and the lake was fully visible now, dimpled by light rain, sweeping away to a dark, distant backcloth of trees. Eleanor felt disembodied, only tenuously present, on loan to this place for a few hours, courtesy of British Airways. She had felt much like that throughout the conference. […]

The meal completed, Eva made a meticulous division of the bill and looked at her watch.

'Excellent – we have still plenty of time. I shall take you to see the waterfall.'

'Well… maybe I should be getting straight to the airport now.'

'No, no. You will only be sitting about there – it is half an hour from here, that is all. And the waterfall is not to be missed. We can drive to a place not far away and then it is a short walk up the mountainside. I have been many times.'

The road climbed up from the lake [...] doubling back on itself in hairpin bends. It was not much more than a track, in any case. The rain had given way now to a thickening mist.

Eleanor said, [...] 'It's going to start getting dark soon, Eva. Are you sure it isn't far?'

'Not far at all. This is the way over here, look… It is a well-known beauty spot.'

But not in the middle of November, thought Eleanor dourly. It was distinctly chilly now and the air was thick with moisture. She tied her scarf around her head and followed Eva up the steep shaly path, slippery from the rain, which wound up between the trees. Eva, in her high-heeled boots, was having difficulty. Eleanor, pointing this out in hopes of a reprieve, was brushed aside. At any moment they would reach the waterfall, Eva assured her. 'Hush… I think I can hear it already.'

For nearly twenty minutes, they scrambled up the mountainside. Then Eva stopped. 'It is possible I have taken the wrong path. I think perhaps we go down some way and see if we have missed a turn.'

Eleanor said, 'I really do feel it would be wise to head for the airport now, Eva.'

'No, no. We are very close, I promise.'

Turning, Eva began a hasty and hazardous descent. Within half a dozen paces she had fallen. Her left foot slipped and twisted and she was on her back on the rain-sodden path.

It was quickly apparent that damage had been done. As soon as Eva tried to get up she became faint. Eleanor squatted beside her on the path, supporting her. 'Just keep still for a minute. You've probably winded yourself.'

'I am all right. Look, I can get up now…' But there was a yelp of pain. 'My ankle…'

'Keep still,' said Eleanor. She improvised a pillow with their two handbags and unzipped Eva's boot. 'Does that hurt?'

It did. And the ankle was beginning to swell. Broken or merely sprained?

'I try to stand,' said Eva. 'Look, it is not so bad…' And immediately fainted.

Eleanor ministered. She found some skin freshener in her handbag and rubbed it on Eva's forehead. Oh God, she thought, what a thing to happen… Presently Eva came to. She stared at Eleanor. 'I am not so good. You will have to take my car and go to get some help. Here – the keys are in my pocket.'

'Eva,' said Eleanor, 'I'm afraid I can't drive.' And have always rather prided myself on the fact, she reflected grimly. Felt myself a touch radical, original. Environmentally chaste.

Eva closed her eyes. 'Ah…' She opened them. 'I am afraid that you may miss your plane.'

'That's the least of it,' said Eleanor heroically. 'The main thing is to get you down from here. Let's try once more and see if you might be able to walk if you lean on me and we take it very slowly.'

They tried. Eva all but passed out again.

'I'm going to have to leave you and find some help,' said Eleanor. Hell and damnation, she thought. [...] She saw the airport departure lounge, the reassuring departure board: BA354 London Heathrow. The light blinking: BOARDING.

'I made perhaps a mistake to go to the waterfall,' said Eva. 'I am sorry, Eleanor. This is most inconvenient for you.' She was now extremely white.

'Never mind. Now look – can you wriggle as far as that pile of leaves there? You'd be a bit more comfortable.'

Eva was laid out by the side of the path. For the second time Eleanor stood looking down at the woman's supine form – the buttoned coat, those boots, her now ashen face. I knew this would happen, thought Eleanor, somehow I knew it. It was built into the day.

Chapter 1: Component 1

SECTION A: 40 marks

*Read carefully the passage in the **separate Resource Material** for use with **Section A**.*

*Then answer **all** the questions below.*

The story in the separate Resource Material is about an English woman called Eleanor who has been attending a conference in Europe.

0 1 **Read lines 1–7.**

List **five** things you learn about Eva in these lines. [5]

0 2 **Read lines 8–38.**

What impressions does the writer create of Eleanor in these lines? [5]

You must refer to the language used in the text to support your answer, using relevant subject terminology where appropriate.

0 3 **Read lines 39–55.**

How does the writer create the sense that something will go wrong in these lines?

You should write about:

- what happens in these lines to suggest that something will go wrong
- the writer's use of language and structure to suggest that something will go wrong [10]

You must refer to the language and structure used in the text to support your answer, using relevant subject terminology where appropriate.

0 4 **Read lines 56–80.**

What are Eleanor's thoughts and feelings in these lines? How does the writer show her thoughts and feelings?

You should write about:

- what happens in these lines
- the writer's use of language [10]

You must refer to the language used in the text to support your answer, using relevant subject terminology where appropriate.

0 5 **To answer this question you need to consider the passage as a whole.**

'The writer presents Eva as reckless and foolish.'

How far do you agree with this view?

You should write about:

- your thoughts and feelings about how Eva is presented in the passage as a whole
- how the writer has created these thoughts and feelings [10]

You must refer to the text to support your answer.

SECTION B: 40 marks

*In this section you will be assessed for the quality of your **creative prose writing** skills.*

24 marks are awarded for communication and organisation; 16 marks are awarded for vocabulary, sentence structure, spelling and punctuation.

You should aim to write about 450–600 words.

Choose **one** of the following titles for your writing: [40]

Either,

a) An Unforgettable Day.

Or,

b) Write a story which begins:

'You could have cut the atmosphere with a knife…'

Or,

c) Write about a time you were envious.

Or,

d) Write a story which ends:

'He knew it had been a mistake to leave his mobile phone on the desk.'

Chapter 1: Component 1

Preparing to practise

Before you try to complete this practice exam paper, you should think carefully about what skills are being tested in each question and how you can best demonstrate those skills. Read through the following information. It will help you to understand each question in the exam paper.

Section A: Question 1

Example Exam Question

> **0 1** Read lines 1–7.
> List **five** things you learn about Eva in these lines.   **[5 marks]**

 You should spend about 5–6 minutes on this question.

What is being tested?

- Your ability to identify and interpret **explicit** and **implicit** information and ideas. (AO1 1a and 1b)

What you have to do

- Using only the lines you have been directed to, you must write down five things that you learn about Eva in lines 1 to 7.

Key terms

explicit: stated clearly and openly

implicit: suggested but not directly expressed

retrieve: to find or extract

Tips

- Make at least five different points in Question 1 in order to gain the full five marks on offer.
- Use the question to frame your answer. For example, 'I learn Eva is…' or 'Eva is…'.
- Use evidence and **retrieve** points directly from the set lines in the text.
- Remember that information may be implied as well as explicitly stated in the text.

Preparing to practise

Section A: Question 2

Example Exam Question

| 0 2 | **Read lines 8–38.**
What impressions does the writer create of Eleanor in these lines? **[5 marks]**

You must refer to the language used in the text to support your answer, using relevant subject terminology where appropriate.

6–7 minutes — You should spend about 6–7 minutes on this question.

What is being tested?

- Your ability to explain, comment on and analyse how writers use language to achieve effects and influence readers, using relevant subject terminology where appropriate. (AO2 1a, c and d)

What you have to do

- Write down your different impressions of Eleanor using evidence to support your answer.
- In this practice question you must focus on lines 8–38.
- Write about how your selected evidence helped to create the impression.
- Analyse the effects of your chosen evidence.

Tips

- Only select evidence and give impressions from the correct lines.
- Remember to explain how impressions of Eleanor are created in the language, rather than just say what they are. This question is assessing how you write about the effects of language.
- Keep in mind that impressions are the ideas and feelings you form about something – in this case the ideas and feelings you have about Eleanor that have been formed by what you have read.
- **Track** through the text **chronologically.** The writer has chosen to put this text together in a particular order – reading it in the order intended and thinking about the choices the writer has made will aid your understanding of meaning.
- Remember to be **specific** rather than **generalised**.
  You need to show a range of impressions – giving one general impression and supporting the same impression with different evidence will not achieve a good mark.
- To access the higher marks in this question, you must focus on specific words and phrases and think about their effects.

Key terms

track: read or follow carefully the progress of the text as it develops

chronologically: in the order in which things occurred

specific: detailed and exact, precise

generalised: making a general statement and not looking at the details

11

Chapter 1: Component 1

Section A: Question 3

Example Exam Question

| 0 3 | **Read lines 39–55.**

How does the writer create the sense that something will go wrong in these lines?

You should write about:
- what happens in these lines to suggest that something will go wrong
- the writer's use of language and structure to suggest that something will go wrong

[10 marks]

You must refer to the language and structure used in the text to support your answer, using relevant subject terminology where appropriate.

> You should spend about 13 minutes on this question.

What is being tested?

- Your ability to explain, comment on and analyse how writers use language and **structure** to achieve effects and influence readers, using relevant subject terminology where appropriate. (AO2 1a, b, c and d)

What you have to do

- In this practice question you must focus on lines 39–55.
- Write about what the writer does to make you think something will go wrong.
- Choose relevant evidence to help you to make your points clearly.
- Analyse the ways that language is used and the way that the text is structured, and the effect this will have on the reader.

Tips

- Underline key words that help you understand the focus of the question and then track through the text chronologically to make sure you don't miss anything.
- Remember to read the italicised text of Questions 2, 3 and 4 of Component 1 extra carefully. They will tell you exactly what to cover in your answer: in this case, you need to look at both language *and* structure.
- Focus on specific words and phrases and think about their effects. Think about the ways in which this helps to create a particular mood or affect the **tone** of the writing.
- Look at the sequencing and structure of the set lines. Consider how the reader moves through the text.

Key terms

structure: the way the text is organised, how it is put together; for example, the writer may use paragraphs, different sentence types and devices such as dialogue deliberately to influence a reader

tone: manner of expression that shows the writer's attitude, e.g. humorous, sarcastic

Section A: Question 4

Example Exam Question

| 0 4 | **Read lines 56–80.**

What are Eleanor's thoughts and feelings in these lines? How does the writer show her thoughts and feelings?

You should write about:

- what happens in these lines
- the writer's use of language

[10 marks]

You must refer to the language used in the text to support your answer, using relevant subject terminology where appropriate.

> You should spend about 13 minutes on this question.

What is being tested?

- Your ability to explain, comment on and analyse how writers use language to achieve effects and influence readers, using relevant subject terminology where appropriate. (AO2 1a, c and d)

What you have to do

- In this practice question you must focus on lines 56–80.
- Write about a range of Eleanor's thoughts and feelings.
- Write about how the language used in your selected evidence reveals Eleanor's thoughts and feelings.
- Analyse the effects of your chosen evidence. In this case, you need to think about how Eleanor's thoughts and feelings are shown through what happens in the text.

Tips

- Keep the focus of the question in mind.
- Make sure you select evidence from the correct lines.
- In this type of question, a character's thoughts and feelings may change or develop so it is sensible to track through the text chronologically to aid your understanding.
- Focus on specific words and phrases, think about their effects and link your explanation clearly to what this says about Eleanor's thoughts and feelings.
- Consider the writer's use of language features and techniques where they are used to communicate Eleanor's thoughts and feelings.
- Remember to be *specific* rather than *generalised*. You need to show a range of different thoughts and feelings.

Chapter 1: Component 1

Section A: Question 5

Example Exam Question

| 0 5 | To answer this question you need to consider the passage as a whole.

'The writer presents Eva as reckless and foolish.'

How far do you agree with this view?

You should write about:

- your thoughts and feelings about how Eva is presented in the passage as a whole
- how the writer has created these thoughts and feelings

[10 marks]

You must refer to the text to support your answer.

> You should spend about 13 minutes on this question.
> **13 minutes**

What is being tested?

- Your ability to **evaluate** texts critically and support this with appropriate textual reference. (AO4)

What you have to do

- In this practice question you must focus on the passage as a whole.
- Decide whether you agree, disagree or partially agree with the statement given and then select relevant evidence from the text to support your ideas.
- Analyse how the evidence helps to support your views.
- Retain a focus on the statement in the question throughout your answer.

Tips

- Remember that Question 5 is assessing your ability to evaluate texts. Evaluation involves writing about the ideas that you form from the text (your thoughts and feelings) and analysing the writer's methods (how you came to reach those ideas).
- Make sure your ideas are presented in relation to the statement in the question and how far you agree with the view presented. Use the phrasing of the question to frame the sentences and evidence in your response, for example, 'Although Eva seems reckless...'.
- A good way to show an alternative view to the statement in the question is to write about other ideas you might have about Eva. This must be clearly linked to evidence but can be a good way of showing there may be more than one way of viewing a character or situation.

Key term

evaluate: to form an opinion after thinking about something carefully

Section B: Question 1

Example Exam Question

Choose **one** of the following titles for your writing:

Either,

1 1   a) An Unforgettable Day.

Or,

1 1   b) Write a story which begins: 'You could have cut the atmosphere with a knife…'

Or,

1 1   c) Write about a time you were envious.

Or,

1 1   d) Write a story which ends: 'He knew it had been a mistake to leave his mobile phone on the desk.'

[40 marks]

 You should spend about 5–10 minutes planning, 30–35 minutes writing and 5 minutes proofreading.

What is being tested?

- Your ability to communicate clearly, effectively and imaginatively, selecting and adapting tone, **style** and **register** for different forms, purposes and audiences. (AO5 1a, b, c)
- Your ability to organise information and ideas, using structural and grammatical features to support coherence and **cohesion** of texts. (AO5 2a, b, c)
- Your ability to use a range of vocabulary and **sentence structures** for clarity, purpose and effect, with accurate spelling and punctuation. (AO6)

What you have to do

- Choose *one* title (or task) from the four given – one from either a, b, c or d.
- Produce a piece of **narrative** writing that engages the reader.
- Demonstrate the ability to communicate clearly, adapt style and tone to the task set. Use vocabulary and **linguistic devices** effectively.
- Structure your writing using paragraphs and organised sentences.

Tips

- Plan how your response will begin and end before you start writing.
- Written accuracy is crucial. Leave time to proofread your work for spelling, punctuation, grammar and clarity.

Key terms

style: the way that something is written or presented

register: the level of formality used in writing or the language used by a particular group of people

cohesion: the quality of being logical and consistent

sentence structure: the way in which the words within a sentence (or sentences) are organised

narrative: a description of events or story

linguistic devices: words or phrases that convey meaning which is different to the literal meaning of the words

 Activity 1 Answering the sample paper

Using all of the skills and techniques suggested on pages 10–15, complete the exam paper on pages 6–9.

15

Chapter 1: Component 1

Understanding the mark scheme

A mark scheme is used by examiners and teachers to assess the quality of your response for each question. Understanding the mark scheme can help you to improve the quality of your work as you will know what is needed to gain the highest marks in each question.

Section A: Question 1

Read the sample Question 1 below from the practice exam paper on pages 6–9.

> **Example Exam Question**
>
> **0 1** Read lines 1–7.
>
> List **five** things you learn about Eva in these lines. **[5 marks]**

This question tests your ability to identify and interpret explicit and implicit information from a text (AO1 1a and b). For Question 1, you are awarded one mark for each correct point that you make, up to a total of five marks.

Mark scheme

Below is the mark scheme for Question 1 of the sample exam paper. It is a list of **indicative content**.

> Award one mark for each point and/or **inference** identified by the candidate, to a maximum of five:
>
> - not everyone likes her – Eleanor was 'not sure'
> - she is a lecturer at the University of Zagreb
> - she is around forty
> - she is 'a somewhat frenzied woman'/excitable
> - she has 'a mane of wiry black hair'
> - she has attached herself to Eleanor
> - she is bossy/has taken control – trip to lake 'at her insistence'
> - she is determined: 'then I take you straight to the airport'
>
> No mark should be awarded for **unabridged quotation** of whole sentences.

Key terms

indicative content: examples of content that examiners will refer to and you may draw upon as part of a successful answer

inference: something that you can find out indirectly from what you already know

unabridged quotation: evidence that is not shortened to focus on what is specifically needed

Improving your Section A: Question 1 response

Activity 2 Self-assessment

1. Mark your original response to Question 1. Using the mark scheme above, decide how many marks you would award yourself for your answer.

Understanding the mark scheme

2. Reread lines 1–7. Using the mark scheme to help you, highlight each thing you learn about Eva in the text. Add any things that you missed about Eva to your original answer.

3. Look at your whole response and see if your mark has improved.

Upgrade

- Make sure that your answer is based on the lines set: in this case, you must focus on lines 1–7.
- You are being tested on your skills of selection. You will not be awarded any marks for points that are copied in full sentences or paragraphs from the text.
- Highlighting or underlining key evidence as you read can help you to focus and reduce the time spent searching for relevant evidence when writing your answer.

Section A: Question 2

Read the sample Question 2 below from the practice exam paper on pages 6–9.

Example Exam Question

02 Read lines 8–38.

What impressions does the writer create of Eleanor in these lines? **[5 marks]**

You must refer to the language used in the text to support your answer, using relevant subject terminology where appropriate.

This question tests your ability to explain, comment on and analyse how writers use language to achieve effects and influence readers, using relevant subject terminology where appropriate (AO2 1a, c and d). Question 2 is assessed using marking bands: each band contains key words and phrases, which examiners use to decide the mark given to a response. These key words and the criteria for each band can be found in the table below.

Band	Marks	Key words/phrases	Explanation
1	1 mark	'limited'	This means that your answer is quite basic and/or very brief.
2	2 marks	'straightforward'	This means your answer is on task but quite simple and undeveloped.
3	3 marks	'some', 'range'	This means your answer shows some successful points and some range but there is more to say.
4	4 marks	'accurate', 'thorough range'	This means you make several correct and/or relevant points and your answer shows some detailed awareness.
5	5 marks	'perceptive', 'well-chosen range'	This means that your answer is precise and shows good insight and awareness. You have selected evidence carefully and convincingly.

Chapter 1: Component 1

Mark scheme

Below is the mark scheme for the sample Question 2 from the practice paper. The key words from each band have been highlighted to help you see how the skills level increases, as progress is made through the bands.

Band 1	Give 1 mark to those who make a very limited response.
Band 2	Give 2 marks to those who identify some straightforward impressions of the character of Eleanor. Subject terminology may be used.
Band 3	Give 3 marks to those who give some impressions of the character of Eleanor and use a range of evidence and language choice to support their answers. These responses may identify some relevant subject terminology, where appropriate.
Band 4	Give 4 marks to those who give accurate impressions of the character of Eleanor and use a thorough range of evidence and language choice to support their answers. Relevant subject terminology may be used accurately to support comments, where appropriate.
Band 5	Give 5 marks to those who make accurate and perceptive comments about the character of Eleanor and use a well-chosen range of evidence and language choice to support their answers. Well-considered, accurate use of relevant subject terminology may support comments effectively.

The mark scheme also includes a list of indicative content. This provides suggested examples of the content that you may include as part of a successful answer to Question 2. This is not a complete list but is a good indicator of the most relevant content for the answer. Below is the indicative content list for the sample Question 2.

> Details candidates may explore or comment on could be:
> - she is reluctant to go to the lake
> - she is not sure about Eva
> - she lacks assertiveness
> - she is well-mannered/abides by social conventions
> - she is willing to make the best of a situation
> - she is suspicious of Eva's motives
> - she feels out of place/not herself at this resort
> - she has felt out of place during her time at the conference
>
> This is not a checklist and the question must be marked in levels of response. Look for and reward valid alternatives.

Sample student responses

Below are extracts from two different answers to this question. The first extract is taken from an answer that was given a mark in Band 3 and the second extract is taken from an answer that was given a mark in Band 5.

Student A

Eleanor lacks assertiveness which we can see because she tried to make 'excuses' to get out of the trip with Eva but didn't put her foot down and refuse to go.

Student B

Eleanor appears to lack any assertiveness or the ability to stand her ground. For example, 'she had made excuses' to avoid the trip with Eva but caved in when Eva, a more forceful character, 'would have none of it'. This impression of Eleanor is cemented through repetition of her thought of 'Never mind'; it appears she is reassuring herself that it's just a matter of going through with it and then she'll be able to be 'home by eleven' which is clearly the place that she actually wants to be.

Understanding the mark scheme

Activity 3 Building levels of response

1. Look at the two sample answers. Student A was awarded a Band 3 mark for the answer and Student B's answer is part of a Band 5 response. What do you think the differences are between these two answers? Complete the following steps:

   a. Underline any impressions given in these answers.

   b. Tick where evidence has been used to support the answer.

   c. Highlight any comments that you think are perceptive.

   d. Circle where subject terminology supports the comments made effectively.

2. Take one of the other examples of indicative content from the list on page 18 (try to select one you didn't include in your original response).

   a. Find a piece of evidence in the text that supports this impression.

   b. Write a brief analysis of this evidence, keeping a clear focus on what impression it creates of Eleanor.

   c. Now review the sentences you have written. Annotate your writing to indicate where you have referred to the question, where you have used evidence from the text, where you have explained your point and where you have used any relevant subject terminology.

Improving your Section A: Question 2 response

Activity 4 Self-assessment

1. Now look at your original response to this question. Compare it to the examples given for Band 3 and Band 5 answers and then use the mark scheme and indicative content on page 18 to decide which band your response fits into.

2. Think about how you could improve your response. Look particularly at the way you have used and analysed the evidence from the text:

   a. Does the evidence you have selected fit the point you are making?

   b. Have you written about what the evidence suggests about Eleanor?

3. Rewrite your response, paying particular attention to the areas you have identified above that could be developed or improved. Check your revised answer against the mark scheme to see if it would now achieve a higher mark.

Upgrade

- Try using phrases such as 'this suggests' or 'this implies' to demonstrate that you are engaging with and trying to interpret the writer's language.
- Think carefully about why a word or phrase has given you a particular impression. For example, the text refers to Eleanor as feeling 'on loan to this place for a few hours'. Think about what the phrase 'on loan' and the limit of only 'a few hours' suggests. Be as precise as you can in your explanation of this.

Chapter 1: Component 1

Section A: Question 3

Read the sample Question 3 below from the practice exam paper on pages 6–9.

Example Exam Question

> **0 3** **Read lines 39–55.**
>
> How does the writer create the sense that something will go wrong in these lines?
>
> You should write about:
>
> - what happens in these lines to suggest that something will go wrong
> - the writer's use of language and structure to suggest that something will go wrong
>
> **[10 marks]**
>
> *You must refer to the language and structure used in the text to support your answer, using relevant subject terminology where appropriate.*

This question tests your ability to explain, comment on and analyse how writers use language and structure to achieve effects and influence readers, using relevant subject terminology where appropriate (AO2 1a, b, c and d). Question 3 is assessed using marking bands: each band contains key words and phrases, which examiners use to decide the mark given to a response. These key words and the criteria for each band can be found in the table below.

Band	Marks	Key words/phrases	Explanation
1	1–2 marks	'identify', 'begin to comment'	This means that you are beginning to find some relevant details and in some cases can make simple points about them.
2	3–4 marks	'straightforward'	This means what that you can find some relevant details and make simple but clear points about them.
3	5–6 marks	'some understanding'	This means you show some awareness of the writer's intended meaning and can give reasons to support your examples.
4	7–8 marks	'accurate', 'range', 'begin to analyse'	This means that you have given a range of precise points and are able to examine the evidence carefully.
5	9–10 marks	'perceptive', 'wide range', 'detailed analysis'	This means that you have made a wide range of observant and insightful points and are able to examine the evidence carefully and thoroughly.

Tip

You may be asked to comment on structure as part of your response to either Question 2, 3 or 4 in the Component 1 exam. The bullet points and italicised text that follow the exam question may indicate whether or not you are expected to analyse structure as part of your answer, so it's important to read the question text carefully.

Understanding the mark scheme

Mark scheme

Below is the mark scheme for the sample Question 3 from the practice paper. The key words from each band have been highlighted to help you see how the skills level increases, as progress is made through the bands.

Band 1	Give 1–2 marks to those who **identify** and **begin to comment** on some examples that suggest things will go wrong.
Band 2	Give 3–4 marks to those who identify and give **straightforward** comments on some examples that suggest things will go wrong. These examples may identify some relevant subject terminology.
Band 3	Give 5–6 marks to those who identify and comment on how a number of different examples suggest things will go wrong and begin to show **some understanding** of how aspects such as language and organisation are used to achieve effects and influence the reader. These responses may begin to use relevant subject terminology accurately to support their comments, where appropriate.
Band 4	Give 7–8 marks to those who make **accurate** comments about how a **range** of different examples suggest things will go wrong and **begin to analyse** how language and the organisation of events are used to achieve effects and influence the reader. Relevant subject terminology is used accurately to support comments effectively, where appropriate.
Band 5	Give 9–10 marks to those who make accurate and **perceptive** comments about how a **wide range** of different examples suggest things will go wrong and provide **detailed analysis** of how language and the organisation of events are used to achieve effects and influence the reader. Subtleties of the writer's technique are explored in relation to how the reader is influenced. Well-considered, accurate use of relevant subject terminology supports comments effectively, where appropriate.

The mark scheme also includes a list of indicative content. This provides suggested examples of the content that you may include as part of a successful answer to Question 3. This is not a complete list, but is a good indicator of the most relevant content for the answer. Below is the indicative content list for the sample Question 3.

Details candidates may explore or comment on could be:

- Eleanor's suggestion she needs to get to the airport
- Eva's confidence in the face of unknown outdoor elements (waterfall, mountain)
- the road they have to travel on is potentially treacherous: 'doubling back on itself'/'hairpin bends'/'not much more than a track'
- the weather is uncertain: 'rain had given way now to a thickening mist'
- darkness is expected soon
- writing structured to release ominous details
- Eleanor's suggestion of doubt – questions distance and time of day
- Eleanor's private thoughts and clarification of it being November
- gradual changes in the weather – becoming 'distinctly chilly' and 'air was thick with moisture'
- description of the path sounds difficult to navigate and increasing sense of danger: 'steep shaly'/'slippery from the rain'/'wound up between the trees'
- inappropriateness of Eva's footwear
- Eleanor's 'hopes of a reprieve' suggest her concern
- they don't reach the waterfall as quickly as expected: still not there after 'twenty minutes' where they 'scrambled'
- becomes clear that they have taken a wrong path
- contrast in attitudes of the two characters

This is not a checklist and the question must be marked in levels of response. Look for and reward valid alternatives.

Chapter 1: Component 1

Sample student responses

Below are extracts from two different answers to this question. The first extract is taken from an answer that was given a mark in Band 1 and the second extract is taken from an answer that was given a mark in Band 4.

Student A

The writer uses many techniques to create the sense that something will go wrong. For example, the writer uses words such as 'climbed', 'hairpin', 'thickening' to create an effect of drama as all of these words are negative and it foreshadows what is to come.

Also we are given the sense that something will go wrong when Eleanor says 'It's going to start getting dark soon, Eva'. This is effective as she says Eva's name which makes the situation seem serious.

Student B

Eva describes the visit to the 'waterfall' as 'not to be missed' but she does seem a little overconfident. Her estimate of 'half an hour from here' and a 'short walk' seem quite vague and optimistic given that they will be going up a 'mountainside'. These doubts are added to with the road they travel by car sounding very treacherous and steep, the writer lists dangerous features such as 'hairpin bends' and the road doubling 'back on itself' which suggests that even before they have left the car they have experienced some extreme countryside. The weather also worsens as the rain gives way to a 'thickening mist' which suggests that they might struggle to see where they are going. The writer uses the weather conditions and the prospect of them worsening further to create a sense of danger which makes it seem like something could go wrong. The combined effect of this and Eleanor saying 'It's going to start getting dark soon' give the impression that both time and the conditions are against them.

Activity 5 Building levels of response

1. Look at the two sample answers. Student A was awarded a Band 1 mark for the answer and Student B's answer is part of a Band 4 response. What are the significant differences in quality between these two answers? Complete the following steps:

    a. Underline any convincing points that have been made.
    b. Tick where supporting evidence has been used correctly.
    c. Highlight any analysis of the evidence that answers the question.
    d. Circle where subject terminology supports the comments made effectively.

2. Student B's answer shows an awareness of structure as it shows how the writer 'lists' dangerous features that they encounter on the road. Look back at the source text on pages 6–7 and analyse any other instances where structure helps to create the sense that something will go wrong. You could explore the sentence structure or how the text begins or ends, and the significance of that.

Understanding the mark scheme

Improving your Section A: Question 3 response

Activity 6 Self-assessment

1. Now look at your original response to this question. Compare it to the examples given for Band 1 and Band 4 answers and then use the mark scheme and indicative content on page 21 to decide which band your response would be awarded.

2. Think about how you could improve your response. Look particularly at the way you have used and analysed the evidence from the text:

   a. Does the evidence you have selected fit the point you are making?

   b. Have you analysed the evidence?

   c. Have you shown clear understanding of how the language and organisation of the text is used to achieve effects and influence the reader?

   d. Have you tracked carefully through the text and found a decent range of points?

   e. Have you used *relevant* subject terminology to further demonstrate your understanding?

   f. Have you considered the advice given in the Upgrade panel?

3. Rewrite your response, paying particular attention to the areas you have identified above that could be developed or improved. Check your revised answer against the mark scheme to see if it would now achieve a higher mark.

Upgrade

- Remember to track through the text – reading the text in chronological order will aid your awareness of the way the writing is sequenced and add to your understanding of structure.
- Think about the possible reasons behind the writer's structural choices and release of information, for example, the use of **dialogue** to increase **tension** and further the narrative.
- It is important to remember the writer makes carefully selected language choices to build to a sense that something could go wrong. For example, Eleanor sounds doubtful and unconvinced by what they are doing. How do phrases like 'Are you sure' and 'in hopes of a reprieve' help to emphasise that?

Key terms

dialogue: the words spoken by people in a piece of writing

tension: a feeling of nervousness, excitement or fear when reading a text

23

Chapter 1: Component 1

Section A: Question 4

Read the sample Question 4 below from the practice exam paper on pages 6–9.

Example Exam Question

> **0 4** **Read lines 56–80.**
>
> What are Eleanor's thoughts and feelings in these lines? How does the writer show her thoughts and feelings?
>
> You should write about:
> - what happens in these lines
> - the writer's use of language
>
> **[10 marks]**
>
> *You must refer to the language used in the text to support your answer, using relevant subject terminology where appropriate.*

This question tests your ability to explain, comment on and analyse how writers use language to achieve effects and influence readers, using relevant subject terminology where appropriate. (AO2 1a, c and d)

Question 4 is assessed using marking bands: each band contains key words and phrases, which examiners use to decide the mark given to a response. These key words and the criteria for each band can be found in the table below.

Key term

omniscient narrator: an 'all-knowing' narrator; a narrator who knows the story's events and character's motives and unspoken thoughts

Band	Marks	Key words/phrases	Explanation
1	1–2 marks	'identify', 'straightforward feelings'	This means that you can locate and present some of Eleanor's more obvious thoughts and feelings.
2	3–4 marks	'identify', 'some understanding'	This means that you can find some of Eleanor's thoughts and feelings and make points about them which show some awareness of the writer's meaning.
3	5–6 marks	'a range', 'begin to analyse'	This means you show awareness of the writer's intended meaning and are starting to examine the evidence. You can do this over a range of examples.
4	7–8 marks	'range', 'detailed analysis'	This means that you have given a range of precise thoughts and feelings and are able to examine the evidence that led you to these points carefully.
5	9–10 marks	'accurate and perceptive', 'subtleties of writer's technique'	This means that you have made a wide range of observant and insightful points about Eleanor's thoughts and feelings. You are able to examine the evidence carefully and thoroughly and distinguish between layers of meaning.

Understanding the mark scheme

Mark scheme

Below is the mark scheme for the sample Question 4 from the practice paper. The key words from each band have been highlighted to help you see how the skills level increases, as progress is made through the bands.

Band 1	Give 1–2 marks to those who **identify** some **straightforward feelings** of Eleanor. Subject terminology may be used.
Band 2	Give 3–4 marks to those who **identify** some of Eleanor's thoughts and feelings and begin to show **some understanding** of how language is used to achieve effects and influence the reader. These responses may identify some subject terminology, where appropriate.
Band 3	Give 5–6 marks to those who give **a range** of Eleanor's thoughts and feelings and **begin to analyse** how language is used to achieve effects and influence the reader. These answers may use relevant subject terminology, where appropriate.
Band 4	Give 7–8 marks to those who give a **range** of Eleanor's thoughts and feelings and provide **detailed analysis** of how language is used to achieve effects and influence the reader. Subject terminology is used accurately, where appropriate.
Band 5	Give 9–10 marks to those who make **accurate and perceptive** comments about Eleanor's thoughts and feelings and provide detailed analysis of how language is used to achieve effects and influence the reader. **Subtleties of the writer's technique** are explored in relation to how the reader is influenced. Well-considered, accurate use of relevant subject terminology supports comments effectively, where appropriate.

The mark scheme also includes a list of indicative content. This provides suggested examples of the content that you may include as part of a successful answer to Question 4. This is not a complete list, but is a good indicator of the most relevant content for the answer. Below is the indicative content list for the sample Question 4.

Details candidates may explore or comment on could be:

- she is keen to head to the airport
- she is quick to try to help Eva: 'squatted beside her'
- she acts/thinks quickly: 'improvised a pillow'
- she is conscious of possible outcomes; the reader gets a sense of her inner questions: 'Broken or merely sprained?'
- she is calm when Eva faints and acts to help: 'Eleanor ministered'
- inwardly, she feels some despair: 'Oh God'
- she has previously prided herself on not being able to drive, but feels some regret now: 'reflected grimly'
- her pride came from feeling that she was 'radical, original' and 'Environmentally chaste'
- she is pragmatic in response to missing the plane: 'That's the least of it'
- she is aware of what is needed: 'The main thing is to get you down'
- she knows she will need to get help: 'I'm going to have to leave you'
- she is inwardly annoyed: 'Hell and damnation'
- she pictures the airport departure board and reflects on what she will be missing
- the dialogue between the two characters helps us to understand Eleanor's thoughts and feelings
- the use of an **omniscient narrator** gives greater insight into her thoughts and feelings
- adverb choices such as 'grimly' and 'heroically'

This is not a checklist and the question must be marked in levels of response. Look for and reward valid alternatives.

Chapter 1: Component 1

Sample student responses

Below are extracts from two different answers to this question. The first extract is taken from an answer that was given a mark in Band 3 and the second extract is taken from an answer that was given a mark in Band 5.

Student A

Eleanor 'squatted beside' Eva which shows she wants to help her. She wonders whether Eva's ankle is 'broken or sprained'. This shows she is being practical and thinking through the possibilities. While she is bringing Eva back around after fainting she thinks 'Oh God' which shows she might be a bit shocked or panicked by what has happened.

Eleanor realises that something she has previously taken pride in – not being able to drive – is not going to work well for them here. She thinks about this 'grimly'. This adverb shows she is quite negative about it.

Student B

The writer's use of adverbs, communicated by an omniscient narrator, to describe Eleanor's speech is helpful in conveying her thoughts and feelings. She is said to reflect 'grimly' on her lack of ability to drive and her previous pride in that fact, which suggests that she is now quite depressed and gloomy about it. She 'heroically' dismisses the idea of missing her plane, as 'the least of it' which demonstrates that she knows that this situation is more urgent than getting to the airport and she has now given up that possibility as lost. The adverb 'heroically' could also suggest that she is responding as the situation demands, but that she feels anything but heroic – if she were to actually give in to her feelings they may be more like the frustrated 'Hell and damnation' that she thinks shortly afterwards as she sets off by herself to find help.

Activity 7 Building levels of response

1. Look at the two sample answers. Student A was awarded a Band 3 mark for the answer and Student B's answer is part of a Band 5 response. What do you think the differences are between these two answers? Complete the following steps:

   a. Underline any thoughts and feelings given in these answers.
   b. Tick where evidence has been used to support the answer.
   c. Highlight any comments that you think are perceptive.
   d. Circle all the points made and decide if a range of different points are covered.

2. Look again at the list of indicative content on page 25. One of the points, towards the end of the list, refers to how the dialogue between the two characters helps us to understand Eleanor's thoughts and feelings.

   a. Select a piece of evidence you could use to explain this point.
   b. Write down two or three sentences in relation to this evidence to show how the dialogue helps us to understand Eleanor's thoughts and/or feelings.
   c. Review the sentences you have written. Annotate your writing to show where you have addressed the question, where you have used evidence from the text and where you have analysed the evidence.

Improving your Section A: Question 4 response

Activity 8 Self-assessment

1. Now look again at your original response to this question. Compare it to the Band 3 and Band 5 answers and then use the mark scheme and indicative content on page 25 to decide which band your response fits into.

2. Think about how you could improve your response. Look particularly at the way you have used and analysed evidence from the text:

   a. Does the evidence you have selected fit the point you are making?

   b. Have you written about Eleanor's thoughts and feelings?

   c. Have you analysed the evidence clearly?

   d. Have you shown clear understanding of how the writer's language is used to achieve effects and influence the reader?

   e. Have you used relevant subject terminology to further demonstrate your understanding? For example, the way the writer uses questions in Eleanor's thoughts ('Broken or merely sprained?') demonstrate her ability to focus on the necessary details in a moment of crisis.

   f. Have you explained the effects of these devices?

3. Rewrite your response, paying particular attention to the areas you have identified above that could be developed or improved. Check your revised answer against the mark scheme to see if it would now achieve a higher mark.

Upgrade

- Remember to track through the text – reading the text in chronological order will aid your awareness of Eleanor's thoughts and feelings and any changes to them.
- Always consider the reasons behind the writer's choices; they will be made for deliberate effect. For example, look at the word 'ministered'. This means that Eleanor attended to Eva's needs and suggests that she is taking very practical action and her thoughts and feelings are driven by what is necessary to do in this situation.

Chapter 1: Component 1

Section A: Question 5

Read the sample Question 5 below from the practice exam paper on pages 6–9.

Example Exam Question

> **0 5** To answer this question you need to consider the passage as a whole.
>
> 'The writer presents Eva as reckless and foolish.'
>
> How far do you agree with this view?
>
> You should write about:
>
> - your thoughts and feelings about how Eva is presented in the passage as a whole
> - how the writer has created these thoughts and feelings
>
> **[10 marks]**
>
> You must refer to the text to support your answer.

This question tests your ability to evaluate texts critically and support this with appropriate textual reference (AO4). Question 5 is assessed using marking bands: each band contains key words and phrases, which examiners use to decide the mark given to a response. These key words and the criteria for each band can be found in the table below.

Band	Marks	Key words/phrases	Explanation
1	1–2 marks	'simple personal opinion', 'linked, basic textual reference'	This means that you can offer a simple view in relation to the character of Eva and the statement in the question and can link this to evidence from the text.
2	3–4 marks	'personal opinion', 'straightforward textual references'	This means that you give clear views in relation to the character of Eva and the statement in the question and are able to support these views with evidence from the text.
3	5–6 marks	'evaluation', 'some critical awareness'	This means that you can express your views and make judgements based on what you have read. You use evidence to support your views. You show some ability to analyse how the evidence has influenced you with regard to Eva's character and are beginning to show an overview of the whole text.
4	7–8 marks	'critical evaluation', 'critical awareness', 'well-selected textual references'	This means that you can express your views and make judgements in an analytical way. You use carefully chosen evidence to support your views about the presentation of Eva's character and are clearly engaged with specific detail as well as the whole text.
5	9–10 marks	'persuasive evaluation', 'perceptive', 'convincing, well selected examples', 'purposeful textual references', 'overview'	This means that you can express convincing views and make judgements in an analytical and insightful way. You use carefully chosen evidence to support your views and are fully engaged by the text. You are able to offer detailed analysis of specifics as well as stand back and write about the presentation of character as a whole.

Understanding the mark scheme

Mark scheme

Below is the mark scheme for the sample Question 5 from the practice paper. The key words from each band have been highlighted to help you see how the skills level increases, as progress is made through the bands.

Band 1	Give 1–2 marks to those who express a **simple personal opinion** with **linked, basic textual reference**.
Band 2	Give 3–4 marks to those who give a **personal opinion** supported by **straightforward textual references**. These responses will show limited interaction with the text as a whole and/or how the writer has created the reader's thoughts and feelings.
Band 3	Give 5–6 marks to those who give an **evaluation** of the text and its effects, supported by appropriate textual references. These responses will show **some critical awareness** of the text as a whole and how the writer has created the reader's thoughts and feelings.
Band 4	Give 7–8 marks to those who give a **critical evaluation** of the text and its effects, supported by **well-selected textual references**. These responses will show **critical awareness** and clear engagement with the text. They will also explore how the writer has created the reader's thoughts and feelings.
Band 5	Give 9–10 marks to those who give a **persuasive evaluation** of the text and its effects, supported by **convincing, well-selected examples** and **purposeful textual references**. These responses will show engagement and involvement, where candidates take an **overview** to make accurate and **perceptive** comments on the text as a whole. They will also explore how the writer has created the reader's thoughts and feelings with insight.

The mark scheme also includes a list of indicative content. This provides suggested examples of the content that you may include as part of a successful answer to Question 5. This is not a complete list, but is a good indicator of the most relevant content for the answer. Below is the indicative content list for the sample Question 5.

Areas for possible evaluation could be:

- **initially she is presented in multiple different ways**
- she is a university lecturer
- she is described as 'somewhat frenzied'
- she attached herself to Eleanor (whether she was wanted or not)
- she is determined to do things her way ('Eva would have none of it')
- she seems manipulative: 'You don't trust me, Eleanor.'
- she wants to talk about applying for a study grant – could be different interpretations
- she is not reckless with money: 'made a meticulous division of the bill'
- **as they head to the waterfall, some of her actions could be reckless or foolish**
- she focuses on the beauty of the surrounding area: 'the waterfall is not to be missed.'
- she seems oblivious to the weather conditions and time of year
- she is inappropriately dressed
- she is falsely convinced of her own knowledge until it becomes clear that they have gone wrong
- she is unwilling to accept defeat
- she rushes to descend ('hasty') and falls
- **at the end Eva is more reflective and the reader is perhaps more sympathetic**
- she realises that things have gone wrong and that she has made mistakes

This is not a checklist and the question must be marked in levels of response. Look for and reward valid alternatives.

Chapter 1: Component 1

Sample student responses

Below are extracts from two different answers to this question. The first extract is taken from an answer that was given a mark in Band 2 and the second extract is taken from an answer that was given a mark in Band 4.

Student A

I agree with this statement as Eva dresses in a way that is not right for the conditions and for going up a mountain. For example, Eva 'in her high-heeled boots, was having difficulty'. It is silly to be going up a mountain in high-heeled boots. She also does not seem to notice that it is going to be getting dark soon and it is Eleanor that tells her this. The writer also makes Eva seem quite bossy and determined to have her own way. She tells Eleanor 'No, no. You will only be sitting about there – it is half an hour from here'. She does not want to take her to the airport and is determined to take her to the waterfall.

Student B

To some extent, I agree that Eva is presented as reckless and foolish. She seems oblivious to the poor weather and conditions, and her choice of 'high-heeled boots' for footwear is inappropriate. This creates the sense that her accident was inevitable. The writer uses the conversation between the two characters to make Eleanor appear sensible and by contrast, Eva as quite foolish. However, Eva is presented in different ways throughout the passage and seems quite a confusing character. She is a university 'lecturer' which probably gives the reader the expectation of her being quite clever. However, she is then described as a 'somewhat frenzied woman'. This adds to the impression of an impulsive person who does things without thinking of them. She seems to use emotional blackmail to get her own way when she says to Eleanor 'you don't trust me'. Eleanor also suspects that she has an ulterior motive in wanting to spend time with her. This presents Eva as more than just reckless and foolish, although she is definitely also both of those things at certain points in the text.

Activity 9 Building levels of response

1. Look at the two sample answers. Student A was awarded a Band 2 mark for the answer and Student B's answer is part of a Band 4 response. What do you think the differences are between these two answers? Complete the following steps:

    a. Underline any examples of personal opinion.
    b. Circle any examples of critical evaluation.
    c. Tick where evidence has been included.
    d. Highlight where evidence has been analysed and note how this is different in each answer.

Understanding the mark scheme

2. Look at the list of indicative content on page 29. The first bullet point is emboldened. This is because it is an overview point and some of the following points can be linked to it.

   a. Choose at least two points from the indicative content that you would use to support this overview point.

   b. Write two or three sentences to analyse your selected evidence and evaluate how this presents Eva as someone who is presented in multiple ways.

   c. Review the sentences you have written. Annotate your writing to show where you have used evidence from the text, where you have analysed the evidence and where you have addressed the question and evaluated how Eva is presented.

Improving your Section A: Question 5 response

Activity 10 Self-assessment

1. Now look again at your original response to Question 5. Compare it to the Band 2 and Band 4 answers and then use the mark scheme and indicative content on page 29 to decide which mark your response would be given.

2. Think about how you could improve your response:

   a. Have you tracked through the text carefully and found a range of points?

   b. Have you explored your thoughts and feelings about Eva?

   c. Have you considered how the writer influences your feelings?

   d. Have you found a clear range of evidence and used it to support your agreement or disagreement with the statement in the question?

   e. Have you considered the points in the upgrade panel?

3. Rewrite your response, paying particular attention to the areas you have identified above that could be developed or improved. Check your revised answer against the mark scheme to see if it would now achieve a higher mark.

Upgrade

- Remember to track through the whole text – reading the text in chronological order will aid the coherence of your answer.
- Focus on what the writer has done to influence your opinions. Look carefully at the writer's language choices and methods. Your opinions about Eva have been influenced by the way the writer has put this text together.
- Consider whether you can make any overview points of how Eva is presented. Drawing together multiple points of evidence in support of a general line of argument will demonstrate your ability to stand back from the text and write about the presentation of the character as a whole.

Chapter 1: Component 1

Section B: Question 1

Read the sample Question 1 below from Section B of the practice exam paper on pages 6–9.

> **Example Exam Question**
>
> Choose **one** of the following titles for your writing:
>
> **Either,**
>
> `1 1`   a) An Unforgettable Day.
>
> **Or,**
>
> `1 1`   b) Write a story which begins: 'You could have cut the atmosphere with a knife…'
>
> **Or,**
>
> `1 1`   c) Write about a time you were envious.
>
> **Or,**
>
> `1 1`   d) Write a story which ends: 'He knew it had been a mistake to leave his mobile phone on the desk.'
>
> [40 marks]

This question tests your ability to communicate your ideas and organise a text effectively (AO5). You need to be able to:

- communicate clearly, effectively and imaginatively, selecting and adapting tone, style and register for different forms, purposes and audiences
- organise information and ideas, using structural and grammatical features to support coherence and cohesion of texts.

This question also tests the accuracy of your vocabulary, sentence structure, spelling and punctuation (AO6). You need to be able to:

- use a range of vocabulary and sentence structures for clarity, purpose and effect, with accurate spelling and punctuation.

Question 1 in Section B of the Component 1 exam paper is worth 40 marks.

The mark scheme is divided into two sections to reflect the two assessment objectives. Of the 40 marks available, the quality of your communication and organisation (AO5) is worth 24 marks, and the quality of your vocabulary, sentence structure, spelling and punctuation (AO6) is worth 16 marks.

Understanding the mark scheme

Communication and Organisation (AO5)

The mark scheme for Communication and Organisation (AO5) is divided into marking bands: each band contains key words and phrases, which examiners use to decide the mark given to a response. These key words and the criteria for each band can be found in the table below.

Band	Key words/phrases	Explanation
1	'basic control and coherence', 'basic organisation', 'communication is limited'	This means that your writing is quite simple and is not always organised in a way that makes sense. You may make some points clearly. Your reader struggles to follow what you have written.
2	'some control and coherence', 'some organisation', 'communication is limited but clear'	This means that your writing is sometimes clear and sometimes makes sense. Your writing is sometimes organised and some ideas make sense and you try to develop them sensibly. You have tried to be clear in the way you put across your ideas but may not always be successful. Sometimes the reader may struggle to understand or lose the sense of what you were trying to say.
3	'mostly controlled and coherent', 'shape and direction', 'communication is clear but limited in ambition'	This means that your writing is mostly clear and mostly makes sense as a whole. You can organise your writing with a sense of purpose and you are generally able to make your meaning clear. Your work may be quite straightforward and not demonstrate the careful crafting of a higher band, but your reader will be able to understand your meaning.
4	'clearly controlled and coherent', 'convincing detail', 'clearly organised', 'some ambition', 'precise meaning'	This means that your writing is clear and makes sense as a whole. You can organise your writing with clarity and you use language carefully to communicate your ideas. Your ideas are consistent, effectively developed and relevant to the task. Your reader is interested by what you write.
5	'fully coherent', 'developed with originality', 'sophisticated', 'fully engages', 'ambitious', 'consistently conveys precise meaning'	This means that your writing has been crafted with confidence and ambition. You know how to structure writing accurately and are willing to be imaginative and sophisticated in your use of language and ideas. You are able to fully engage your reader and make sure that they are emotionally involved in the narrative.

Below, and on page 34, is the mark scheme for Communication and Organisation (AO5) for Section B: Question 1 of the practice paper on pages 6–9. The key words from each band have been highlighted to help you see how the skills level increases, as progress is made through the bands.

Band 1	**1–4 marks** • there is basic control and coherence (a basic sense of plot and characterisation) • there is basic organisation (paragraphs may be used to show obvious divisions) • there is some use of structure and grammatical features to convey meaning • communication is limited but some meaning is conveyed
Band 2	**5–9 marks** • there is some control and coherence (some control of plot and characterisation) • there is some organisation (narrative is beginning to have some shape and development) • structure and grammatical features are used to convey meaning • communication is limited but clear

Chapter 1: Component 1

Band 3	**10–14 marks** • the writing is mostly controlled and coherent (plot and characterisation show some detail and development) • the writing is organised (narrative has shape and direction) • structure and grammatical features are used with some accuracy to convey meaning • communication is clear but limited in ambition
Band 4	**15–19 marks** • the writing is clearly controlled and coherent (plot and characterisation show convincing detail and some originality and imagination) • the writing is clearly organised (narrative is purposefully shaped and developed) • structure and grammatical features are used accurately to support cohesion and coherence • communication shows some ambition and conveys precise meaning
Band 5	**20–24 marks** • the writing is fully coherent and controlled (plot and characterisation are developed with detail, originality and imagination) • the writing is clearly and imaginatively organised (narrative is sophisticated and fully engages the reader's interest) • structure and grammatical features are used ambitiously to give the writing cohesion and coherence • communication is ambitious and consistently conveys precise meaning

Vocabulary, Sentence structure, Spelling and Punctuation (AO6)

The mark scheme for Vocabulary, Sentence structure, Spelling and Punctuation (AO6) is also divided into five marking bands: each band contains key words and phrases, which examiners use to decide the mark given to a response. These key words and the criteria for each band can be found in the table below.

Band	Key words/phrases	Explanation
1	'limited range', 'limited control', 'some attempt to use…'	This means that your writing is not very accurate. Your spelling and use of punctuation and grammar contain basic errors that hinder the meaning and/or your sentences lack variety. If you were to underline all of the errors in your work there would probably be a lot of areas underlined in your writing.
2	'some variety', 'some control', 'usually accurate', 'generally secure', 'some range'	This means that your writing is sometimes accurate. Spelling, punctuation and grammar are sometimes controlled but there will be some errors across multiple areas (for example, in spelling, punctuation and grammar). Your use of vocabulary shows some range but this may be simple and/or have mixed success.
3	'variety in sentence structure', 'mostly secure', 'mostly accurate', 'beginning to develop'	This means that your writing is mostly accurate and reliable. Spelling, punctuation and grammar are mostly controlled. Your use of vocabulary is beginning to show care and some thought.
4	'varied', 'secure', 'range'	This means that your writing is generally very accurate and reliable. Spelling, punctuation and grammar are accurate and care has been taken. Your use of vocabulary is careful and thoughtful.
5	'appropriate and effective variation', 'controlled and accurate', 'confidently', 'totally secure', 'wide range', 'ambitious'	This means that your writing is extremely accurate. Errors rarely occur and your writing is technically sophisticated and carefully crafted for effect. You can use a wide range of carefully chosen vocabulary for maximum effect.

Understanding the mark scheme

Below is the mark scheme for Vocabulary, Sentence structure, Spelling and Punctuation (AO6) for Section B: Question 1 of the practice paper on pages 6–9. The key words from each band have been highlighted to help you see how the skills level increases, as progress is made through the bands.

Band 1	**1–3 marks** • limited range of sentence structure • control of sentence construction is limited • there is some attempt to use punctuation • some spelling is accurate • control of tense and agreement is limited • limited range of vocabulary
Band 2	**4–6 marks** • some variety of sentence structure • there is some control of sentence construction • some control of a range of punctuation • the spelling is usually accurate • control of tense and agreement is generally secure • there is some range of vocabulary
Band 3	**7–10 marks** • there is variety in sentence structure • control of sentence construction is mostly secure • a range of punctuation is used, mostly accurately • most spelling, including that of irregular words, is correct • control of tense and agreement is mostly secure • vocabulary is beginning to develop and is used with some precision
Band 4	**11–13 marks** • sentence structure is varied to achieve particular effects • control of sentence construction is secure • a range of punctuation is used accurately • spelling, including that of irregular words, is secure • control of tense and agreement is secure • vocabulary is ambitious and used with precision
Band 5	**14–16 marks** • there is appropriate and effective variation of sentence structures • virtually all sentence construction is controlled and accurate • a range of punctuation is used confidently and accurately • virtually all spelling, including that of complex irregular words, is correct • control of tense and agreement is totally secure • a wide range of appropriate, ambitious vocabulary is used to create effect or convey precise meaning

Chapter 1: Component 1

Improving your Section B: Question 1 response

Activity 11 Self-assessment

1. Now read your original response to Section B: Question 1. Refer back to the mark scheme for Communication and Organisation (AO5) on pages 33–34. Decide which mark your response would be given.

2. Think about how you could improve your response. Consider the points below:

   Organisation:
   - Did you write a plan to help you organise your thinking and work out the sequencing of your narrative?
   - Is your plot coherent and are characters developed convincingly?
   - Have you linked your ideas convincingly?
   - Have you paragraphed your writing effectively?
   - Is your writing relevant to the task?

   Communication:
   - Have you written in sufficient detail?
   - Have you worked to engage your reader? For example, through the use of questions, humour or even comments directed specifically to the reader.
   - Have you thought carefully about vocabulary and how you could use linguistic devices?
   - If you were instructed to write with a particular ending or beginning in mind have you achieved this?

3. Now refer to the mark scheme for Vocabulary, Sentence structure, Spelling and Punctuation (AO6) on page 35. Review each sentence of your writing, and decide which mark your response would be given for this mark scheme.

4. Think about how your technical accuracy could be improved. Read your writing in detail and check the following:

   a. Have you made any frequent spelling errors?
   b. Have you copied down all spellings accurately from the exam paper?
   c. Have you used a range of different punctuation types, for example, full stops, questions marks and commas?
   d. Have you used **tenses** and verb agreement correctly in your writing?
   e. Have you varied the length and order of your sentences?

36

Understanding the mark scheme

5. Rewrite your response, paying particular attention to the areas you have identified above that could be developed or improved, as well as the Upgrade advice. Check your revised answer against the mark scheme to see if it would now achieve a higher mark.

Upgrade

- Think carefully about the plot of your writing, including the way that you sequence events. Are you going to include an interesting opening or ending? How could you create an immediate **atmosphere** or build the narrative to a point of tension? Could you include plot devices, like dialogue or flashbacks?
- Consider how you want your story to be read; give your reader a clear **perspective** (using **first person** or third person) or use an omniscient narrator to give the reader an insight.
- Take the time to add colour and interest to your story through the setting and mood and closely-observed detail that will capture your reader's interest.
- Make decisions about the key characters in the story, and focus on their emotions and behaviour to achieve effects.
- Plan your writing thoroughly. A plan will help you to think through all of these elements and make sure that your ideas are well organised before you begin to write.
- Remember you want your reader to understand what you are writing. Check your writing for spelling, punctuation and grammar, as well as use of the correct tense, which can often cause meaning to break down. If you start writing in one tense, use it consistently throughout your writing.

Key terms

tenses: the form of verbs used to show the time of the action, in the past, present or future

atmosphere: the feeling or mood of a particular place or situation

perspective: a particular attitude towards something or way of regarding something; a point of view

first person: when we use 'I' or 'we' as the narrative voice in a text

Chapter 2: Component 1

Component 1 sample exam paper

This story is set on the day that World War Two was announced. It is about a young woman called Margaret who lives with her family.

Margaret Oxenford was outside the sprawling brick mansion that was her family home, perspiring gently in a hat and coat and fuming because she was forced to go to church. On the far side of the village the single bell in the church tower tolled a monotonous note.　　1

Margaret hated church, but her father would not let her miss the service, even though she was nineteen and old enough to make up her own mind about religion.　　5

A year or so ago she had summoned up the nerve to tell him that she did not want to go, but he had refused to listen. Margaret had said, 'Don't you think it's hypocritical for me to go to church when I don't believe in God?' Father had replied, 'Don't be ridiculous.' Defeated and angry, she had told her mother that when she was of age she would never go to church again. Mother had said, 'That will be up to your husband, dear.' As far as they were concerned the argument was　　10
over, but Margaret had seethed with resentment every Sunday morning since then. […]

Margaret dreaded war. A boy she loved had died in the Spanish Civil War. It was just over a year ago, but she still cried sometimes at night. To her, war meant that thousands more girls would know the grief she had suffered. The thought was almost unbearable.

And yet another part of her wanted war. For years she had felt strongly about Britain's　　15
cowardice during the Spanish war. […] If Britain would now take a stand against the Fascists she could begin to feel proud of her country again.

There was another reason why her heart leapt at the prospect of war. It would surely mean the end of the narrow, suffocating life she lived with her parents. She was bored, cramped and frustrated by their unvarying rituals and their pointless social life. She longed to escape and have a life of her　　20
own, but it seemed impossible: she was under age, she had no money, and there was no kind of work that she was fit for. But, she thought eagerly, surely everything would be different in wartime?

She had read with fascination how in the last war women had put on trousers and gone to work in factories. Nowadays there were female branches of the army, navy and air force. Margaret dreamed of volunteering for the Auxiliary Territorial Service, the women's army. One of the few practical skills　　25
she possessed was that she could drive […] and Ian, the boy who had died, had let her ride his motorcycle. She could even handle a motor boat, for Father kept a small yacht at Nice. […]

War was declared during the service, they found out later. […] So the Oxenhope family walked home from church unaware that they were at war with Germany. […] They took off their hats and went into the morning room. Father turned on the wireless, and it was then that they heard　　30
the news: Britain had declared war on Germany.

Margaret felt a kind of savage glee rising in her breast, like the excitement of driving too fast or climbing to the top of a tall tree. There was no longer any point in agonising over it: there would be tragedy and bereavement, pain and grief, but now these things could not be avoided, the die was cast and the only thing to do was fight. […]　　35

Father said grace and they sat down. Bates offered Mother the smoked salmon. […] 'Of course, there's only one thing to be done,' Mother said as she helped herself from the proffered plate. She spoke in the offhand tone of one who merely draws attention to the obvious. 'We must all go and live in America until this silly war is over.'

There was a moment of shocked silence. Margaret, horrified, burst out, 'No!'　　40

Mother said, 'Now, I think we've had quite enough squabbling for one day. Please let us have lunch in peace and harmony.'

'No!' Margaret repeated. She was almost speechless with outrage. 'You – you can't do this, it's – it's –' She wanted to rail and storm at them, […] to shout her contempt and defiance out loud, but the words would not come, and all she could say was, 'It's not fair!'

Even that was too much. Father said, 'If you can't hold your tongue, you'd better leave us.'

Margaret put her napkin to her mouth to choke down a sob, […] and fled the room. […]

All day Monday she felt unable to eat. She drank endless cups of tea while the servants went about the business of closing up the house. On Tuesday, when Mother realised that Margaret was not going to pack, she told the new maid, Jenkins, to do it for her. Of course, Jenkins did not know what to pack, and Margaret had to help her; so in the end Mother got her way, as she so often did.

Margaret said to the girl, 'It's bad luck for you that we decided to close up the house the week after you started work here.'

'There'll be no shortage of work now, m'lady,' Jenkins said. 'Our dad says there's no unemployment in wartime. […] I'm going to join up. It said on the wireless that seventeen thousand women joined the ATS yesterday.' […]

'What does your dad say about you joining up?'

'I shan't tell him – just do it.'

'But what if he takes you back?'

'He can't do that. I'm eighteen. Once you've signed on, that's it. Provided you're old enough there's nothing your parents can do about it.'

Margaret was startled. 'Are you sure?'

'Course. Everyone knows.'

'I didn't,' Margaret said thoughtfully. […]

Margaret realised that she was going to spend the war in Connecticut unless she did something other than sulk. Despite Mother's plea not to make a fuss, she had to confront her father.

The very thought made her feel shaky. She went back to her room to steel her nerves and consider what she might say. She would have to be calm. Tears would not move him and anger would only provoke his scorn. She should appear sensible, responsible, mature. She should not be argumentative, for that would enrage him […].

She could live with relatives until she joined up, which would be a matter of days. She was nineteen: […] old enough to get married, drive a car, and go to jail. There was no reason why she should not be allowed to stay in England.

That made sense. Now all she needed was courage.

Father would be in his study with his business manager. Margaret left her room. […]

The housekeeper rustled across the hall in her black silk dress. Mrs Allen ruled the female staff of the household strictly, but she had always been indulgent towards the children. She was […] upset that they were leaving: it was the end of a way of life for her. She gave Margaret a tearful smile.

Looking at her, Margaret was struck by a heart-stopping notion.

An entire plan of escape came full-blown into her head. She would borrow money from Mrs Allen, leave the house now, catch the four fifty-five train to London, stay overnight at her cousin Catherine's flat, and join the ATS first thing in the morning. By the time Father caught up with her it would be too late.

Chapter 2: Component 1

SECTION A: 40 Marks

*Read carefully the passage in the **separate Resource Material** for use with **Section A**.*

*Then answer **all** the questions below.*

The story in the separate Resource Material is set at the beginning of World War Two. It is about a young woman called Margaret who lives with her family.

0 1   **Read lines 1–5.**

List **five** things you learn about Margaret in these lines. [5]

0 2   **Read lines 6–22.**

What impressions does the writer create of the Oxenford family in these lines? [5]

You must refer to the language used in the text to support your answer, using relevant subject terminology where appropriate.

0 3   **Read lines 23–47.**

How does the writer show the different reactions of the Oxenford family to the news of war?

You should write about:

- what the Oxenford family members say and do in these lines
- the writer's use of language and structure to show their reactions [10]

You must refer to the language and structure used in the text to support your answer, using relevant subject terminology where appropriate.

0 4   **Read lines 48–75.**

What are Margaret's thoughts and feelings in these lines? How does the writer show her thoughts and feelings?

You should write about:

- what happens in these lines
- the writer's use of language [10]

You must refer to the language used in the text to support your answer, using relevant subject terminology where appropriate.

0 5   **To answer this question you need to read lines 76-84 and also consider the passage as whole.**

'The writer presents Margaret as someone who has no choice but to act on impulse.'

How far do you agree with this view?

You should write about:

- your thoughts and feelings about how Margaret is presented in the passage as a whole
- how the writer has created these thoughts and feelings [10]

You must refer to the text to support your answer.

SECTION B: 40 marks

*In this section you will be assessed for the quality of your **creative prose writing** skills.*

24 marks are awarded for communication and organisation; 16 marks are awarded for vocabulary, sentence structure, spelling and punctuation.

You should aim to write about 450–600 words.

Choose **one** of the following titles for your writing: [40]

Either,

a) The discovery.

Or,

b) Write a story which begins:
   'I kept hoping that the phone would ring…'

Or,

c) Write about a time when you were ashamed of yourself.

Or,

d) The new arrival.

Chapter 2: Component 1

Preparing to practise

Before you try to complete this practice exam paper, you should think carefully about what skills are being tested in each question and how you can best demonstrate those skills. Read through the following information. It will help you to understand each question in the exam paper.

Section A: Question 1

Example Exam Question

> **0 1** Read lines 1–5.
>
> List **five** things you learn about Margaret in these lines.
>
> [5 marks]

You should spend about 5–6 minutes on this question.

What is being tested?

- Your ability to identify and interpret explicit and implicit information and ideas. (AO1 1a and 1b)

What you have to do

- Using only the lines you have been directed to, you must write down five things that you learn about Margaret in lines 1–5.

Tips

- Make at least five different points in Question 1 in order to gain the full five marks on offer.
- Use the question to frame your answer. For example, 'I learn Margaret is…' or 'Margaret is…'.
- Use evidence and retrieve points directly from the set lines in the text.
- Remember that information may be implied as well as explicitly stated in the text.

Preparing to practise

Section A: Question 2

Example Exam Question

> **0 2**   **Read lines 6–22.**
>
> What impressions does the writer create of the Oxenford family in these lines?
>
> **[5 marks]**
>
> *You must refer to the language used in the text to support your answer, using relevant subject terminology where appropriate.*

You should spend about 6–7 minutes on this question.

What is being tested?

- Your ability to explain, comment on and analyse how writers use language to achieve effects and influence readers, using relevant subject terminology where appropriate. (AO2 1a, c and d)

What you have to do

- Write down your impressions of the Oxenford family as a whole or different members of the Oxenford family and how they behave towards one another. Use evidence to support your answer. In this practice question you must focus on lines 6–22.
- Write about how your selected evidence helped to create the impression.
- Analyse the effects of your chosen evidence.

Tips

- Only select evidence and give impressions from the correct lines.
- Remember to explain how impressions of the Oxenford family are created in the language, rather than just say what they are. This question is assessing how you write about the effects of language.
- Keep in mind that impressions are the ideas and feelings you form about something – in this case the ideas and feelings you have about the family as a whole, as well as about the different members of the family. These impressions will all have been formed by what you have read.
- Track through the text chronologically. The writer has chosen to put this text together in a particular order – reading it in the order intended and thinking about the choices the writer has made will aid in your understanding of meaning.
- Remember to be specific rather than generalised.

   You need to show a range of impressions – giving one general impression and supporting the same impression with different evidence will not achieve a good mark.

- To access the higher marks in this question, you must focus on specific words and phrases and think about their effects.

Chapter 2: Component 1

Section A: Question 3

Example Exam Question

> **0 3** **Read lines 23–47.**
>
> How does the writer show the different reactions of the Oxenford family to the news of war?
>
> You should write about:
> - what the Oxenford family members say and do in these lines
> - the writer's use of language and structure to show their reactions
>
> **[10 marks]**
>
> *You must refer to the language and structure used in the text to support your answer, using relevant subject terminology where appropriate.*

You should spend about 13 minutes on this question.

What is being tested?

- Your ability to explain, comment on and analyse how writers use language and structure to achieve effects and influence readers, using relevant subject terminology where appropriate. (AO2 1a, b, c and d)

What you have to do

- In this practice question you must focus on lines 23–47.
- Write about what the writer does to show you the different reactions of the family members.
- Choose relevant evidence to help you to make your points clearly and with focus.
- Analyse the ways that language is used and the way that the text is structured, and the effect this will have on the reader.

Tips

- Underline key words that help you understand the focus of the question. In this case you need to focus on how the writer shows us the different reactions of the individual family members to the news that the nation is at war. Track through the text chronologically to make sure you don't miss anything.

- Remember to read the italicised text of Questions 2, 3 and 4 of Component 1 extra carefully. They will tell you exactly what to cover in your answer: in this case, you need to look at both language *and* structure.

Preparing to practise

Section A: Question 4

Example Exam Question

> **0 4** **Read lines 48–75.**
>
> What are Margaret's thoughts and feelings in these lines? How does the writer show her thoughts and feelings?
>
> You should write about:
> - what happens in these lines
> - the writer's use of language
>
> **[10 marks]**
>
> *You must refer to the language used in the text to support your answer, using relevant subject terminology where appropriate.*

You should spend about 13 minutes on this question.

What is being tested?

- Your ability to explain, comment on and analyse how writers use language to achieve effects and influence readers, using relevant subject terminology where appropriate. (AO2 1a, c and d)

What you have to do

- In this practice question you must focus on lines 48–75.
- Write about a range of Margaret's thoughts and feelings.
- Write about how the language used in your selected evidence reveals Margaret's thoughts and feelings.
- Analyse the effects of your chosen evidence. In this case, you may need to think about how Margaret's thoughts and feelings are shown through what happens in the text.

Tips

- Keep the focus of the question in mind.
- Make sure you select evidence from the correct lines.
- In this type of question, a character's thoughts and feelings may change or develop so it is sensible to track through the text chronologically to aid your understanding.
- Focus on specific words and phrases, think about their effects and link your explanation clearly to what this says about Margaret's thoughts and feelings.
- Consider the writer's use of language features and techniques where they are used to communicate Margaret's thoughts and feelings.
- Remember to be *specific* rather than *generalised*. You need to show a range of different thoughts and feelings.
- Look at the sequencing and structure of the set lines. Consider how the reader moves through the text.

45

Chapter 2: Component 1

Section A: Question 5

Example Exam Question

| 0 5 | To answer this question you need to read lines 76–84 and also consider the passage as whole.

'The writer presents Margaret as someone who has no choice but to act on impulse.'

How far do you agree with this view?

You should write about:

- your thoughts and feelings about how Margaret is presented in the passage as a whole
- how the writer has created these thoughts and feelings

[10 marks]

You must refer to the text to support your answer.

> You should spend about 13 minutes on this question.

What is being tested?

- Your ability to evaluate texts critically and support this with appropriate textual references. (AO4)

What you have to do

- In this practice question you must focus on the passage as a whole.
- Decide whether you agree, disagree or partially agree with the statement given and then select relevant evidence from the text to support your ideas.
- Support your evaluation with a range of evidence that suggests Margaret is (or is not) someone who has no choice but to act on impulse.
- Analyse how the evidence helps to support your views.
- Retain a focus on the statement in the question throughout your answer.

Tips

- Remember that Question 5 is assessing your skills of evaluating texts. Evaluation involves writing about the ideas that you form from the text (your thoughts and feelings) and analysing the writer's methods (how you came to reach those ideas).

- Make sure that your ideas are presented in relation to the statement in the question and how far you agree with the view presented. Use the phrasing of the question to frame the sentences and evidence in your response, for example 'Margaret is sometimes presented as someone who acts…'.

- A good way to show an alternative view to the statement in the question is to write about other ideas you might have about Margaret. This must be clearly linked to evidence but can be a good way of showing there may be more than one way of viewing a character or situation.

46

Preparing to practise

Section B: Question 1

Example Exam Question

Choose **one** of the following titles for your writing:

Either,

| 1 | 1 | a) The discovery.

Or,

| 1 | 1 | b) Write a story which begins: 'I kept hoping that the phone would ring…'

Or,

| 1 | 1 | c) Write about a time when you were ashamed of yourself.

Or,

| 1 | 1 | d) The new arrival.

[40 marks]

You should spend about 5–10 minutes planning, 30–35 minutes writing and 5 minutes proofreading. (45 minutes)

What is being tested?

- Your ability to communicate clearly, effectively and imaginatively, selecting and adapting tone, style and register for different forms, purposes and audiences. (AO5 1a, b, c)
- Your ability to organise information and ideas, using structural and grammatical features to support coherence and cohesion of texts. (AO5 2a, b, c)
- Your ability to use a range of vocabulary and sentence structures for clarity, purpose and effect, with accurate spelling and punctuation. (AO6)

What you have to do

- Choose *one* title (or task) from the four given – one from either a, b, c or d.
- Produce a piece of narrative writing that engages the reader.
- Demonstrate the ability to communicate clearly and adapt style and tone to the task set. Use vocabulary and linguistic devices effectively.
- Structure your writing using paragraphs and organised structured sentences.

Tips

- Remember that you are being assessed on the quality of your writing. Clear communication with your reader is essential.
- Written accuracy is crucial. Leave time to proofread your work for spelling, punctuation, grammar and clarity.

✏ Activity 1 Answering the sample paper

Using all of the skills and techniques suggested on pages 42–47, complete the exam paper on pages 38–41.

47

Chapter 2: Component 1

Understanding the mark scheme

A mark scheme is used by examiners and teachers to assess the quality of your response to each question. Understanding the mark scheme can help you to improve the quality of your work as you will know what is needed to gain the highest marks in each question.

Section A: Question 1

Read the sample Question 1 below from the practice exam paper on pages 38–41.

> **Example Exam Question**
>
> **0 1** **Read lines 1–5.**
>
> List **five** things you learn about Margaret in these lines.
>
> **[5 marks]**

This question tests your ability to identify and interpret explicit and implicit information from a text (AO1 1a and b). For Question 1, you are awarded one mark for each correct point that you make, up to a total of five marks.

Mark scheme

Below is the mark scheme for Question 1 of the sample exam paper. It is a list of indicative content.

> Award one mark for each point and/or inference identified by the candidate, to a maximum of five:
>
> - she is standing outside her house
> - she lives in a 'sprawling brick mansion'
> - she was quite warm: 'perspiring gently'
> - she is angry ('fuming') because she was 'forced to go to church'
> - she hates church
> - she is controlled by her father
> - she is nineteen
>
> No mark should be awarded for unabridged quotation of whole sentences.

Improving your Section A: Question 1 response

Activity 2 Self-assessment

1. Mark your original response to Question 1. Using the mark scheme above, decide how many marks out of five you would award yourself for your answer.

2. Reread lines 1–5. Using the mark scheme to help you, highlight each thing you learn about Margaret in the text. Add any things that you missed about Margaret to your original answer.

3. Look at your whole response and see if your mark has improved.

Understanding the mark scheme

> **Upgrade**
>
> - Make sure that your answer is based on the lines set. You will not be awarded marks for points that are made from other areas of the text.
> - Your point can be made about something explicitly referred to in the text or something that you have inferred from implicit detail.
> - It's important to remember that the points you select must be relevant – they must answer the question. In this case, that means your points must state what you have learned about Margaret.
> - You are being tested on your skills of selection. You will not be awarded any marks for points that are copied in full sentences or paragraphs from the text.
> - Highlighting or underlining key evidence as you read can help you to focus and reduce the time spent searching for relevant evidence when writing your answer.

Section A: Question 2

Read the sample Question 2 below from the practice exam paper on pages 38–41.

Example Exam Question

> **0 2** Read lines 6–22.
>
> What impressions dos the writer create of the Oxenford family in these lines?
>
> **[5 marks]**
>
> *You must refer to the language used in the text to support your answer, using relevant subject terminology where appropriate.*

This question tests your ability to explain, comment on and analyse how writers use language to achieve effects and influence readers, using relevant subject terminology where appropriate (AO2 1a, c and d). Question 2 is assessed using marking bands: each band contains key words and phrases, which examiners use to decide the mark given to a response. These key words and the criteria for each band can be found in the table below.

Band	Marks	Key words/phrases	Explanation
1	1 mark	'limited'	This means that your answer is quite basic and/or very brief.
2	2 marks	'straightforward'	This means your answer is on task but quite simple and undeveloped.
3	3 marks	'some'	This means your answer shows some successful points and some range but there is more to say.
4	4 marks	'accurate', 'thorough range'	This means you make several correct and/or relevant points and your answer shows some detailed awareness.
5	5 marks	'perceptive', 'well-chosen range'	This means that your answer is precise and shows good insight and awareness. You have selected evidence carefully and convincingly.

Chapter 2: Component 1

Mark scheme

Below is the mark scheme for the sample Question 2 from the practice paper. The key words from each band have been highlighted to help you see how the skills level increases, as progress is made through the bands.

Band 1	Give 1 mark to those who make a very **limited** response.
Band 2	Give 2 marks to those who identify some **straightforward** impressions of the Oxenford family. Subject terminology may be used.
Band 3	Give 3 marks to those who give **some** impressions of the Oxenford family and use a range of evidence and language choice to support their answers. These responses may identify some relevant subject terminology, where appropriate.
Band 4	Give 4 marks to those who give **accurate** impressions of the Oxenford family and use a **thorough range** of evidence and language choice to support their answers. Relevant subject terminology may be used accurately to support comments, where appropriate.
Band 5	Give 5 marks to those who make accurate and **perceptive** comments about the Oxenford family and use a **well-chosen range** of evidence and language choice to support their answers. Well-considered, accurate use of relevant subject terminology may support comments effectively.

The mark scheme also includes a list of indicative content. This provides suggested examples of the content that you may include as part of a successful answer to Question 2. This is not a complete list but is a good indicator of the most relevant content for the answer. Below is the indicative content list for the sample Question 2.

> Details candidates may explore or comment on could be:
> - Margaret seems intimidated by her father
> - her father is unwilling to listen
> - Margaret has a problematic relationship with her father
> - Margaret's mother has old-fashioned/traditional views
> - Margaret feels that her life with her parents is boring/suffocating
> - their family life lacks variety and consists of 'unvarying rituals' and 'pointless social life'
> - Margaret longs for escape and 'a life of her own'
> - war might offer her a way out and force change upon the family
>
> This is not a checklist and the question must be marked in levels of response. Look for and reward valid alternatives.

Sample student responses

Below are extracts from two different answers to this question. The first extract is taken from an answer that was given a mark in Band 3 and the second extract is taken from an answer that was given a mark in Band 5.

Student A

> Margaret's mother seems to have outdated views and tells her that when she is 'of age' Margaret's decisions will be 'up to your husband', which is a very traditional way of looking at things.

Student B

> The Oxenford family seem to be very traditional with the father ruling the household with the mother's support. They seem to expect Margaret to fall in line with their rules and thinking until she is married. When she tells her mother she will 'never go to church again' when she is 'of age', her mother tells her 'that will be up to' her husband. It seems that Margaret's mother's views are indistinguishable from those of her father and represented by the collective 'they', as in 'as far as they were concerned the argument was over'.

Understanding the mark scheme

Activity 3 Building levels of response

1. Look at the two sample answers. Student A was awarded a Band 3 mark for the answer and Student B's answer is part of a Band 5 response. What are the key differences between these two answers? Complete the following steps:

   a. Underline any impressions given in these answers.
   b. Tick where evidence has been used to support the answer.
   c. Highlight any comments that you think are perceptive.
   d. Circle where subject terminology supports the comments made effectively.

2. Take one of the other examples of indicative content from the list on page 50.

   a. Find a piece of evidence in the text that supports this impression.
   b. Write a brief analysis of this evidence, keeping a clear focus on what impression it creates of Margaret.
   c. Now review the sentences you have written. Annotate your writing to indicate where you have referred to the question, where you have used evidence from the text, where you have explained your point and where you have used any relevant subject terminology.

Improving your Section A: Question 2 response

Activity 4 Self-assessment

1. Now look at your original response to this question. Compare it to the examples given for Band 3 and Band 5 answers and then use the mark scheme and indicative content on page 50 to decide which band your response fits into.

2. Think about how you could improve your response. Look particularly at the way you have used and analysed the evidence from the text:

   a. Does the evidence you have selected fit the point you are making?
   b. Have you written about what the evidence suggests about the Oxenford family?

3. Rewrite your response, paying particular attention to the areas you have identified above that could be developed or improved. Check your revised answer against the mark scheme to see if it would now achieve a higher mark.

Upgrade

- Try using phrases such as 'this suggests' or 'this implies' to demonstrate that you are engaging with and trying to interpret the writer's language.
- Think carefully about why a word or phrase has given you a particular impression. For example, the text tells us that Margaret feels 'bored, cramped and frustrated' by life with her parents. Think about what these words suggest and what the impact is of them being used together.

51

Chapter 2: Component 1

Section A: Question 3

Read the sample Question 3 below from the practice exam paper on pages 38–41.

Example Exam Question

> **0 3** Read lines 23–47.
>
> How does the writer show the different reactions of the Oxenford family to the news of war?
>
> You should write about:
>
> - what the Oxenford family members say and do in these lines
> - the writer's use of language and structure to show their reactions
>
> **[10 marks]**
>
> *You must refer to the language and structure used in the text to support your answer, using relevant subject terminology where appropriate.*

This question tests your ability to explain, comment on and analyse how writers use language and structure to achieve effects and influence readers, using relevant subject terminology where appropriate (AO2 1a, b, c and d). Question 3 is assessed using marking bands: each band contains key words and phrases, which examiners use to decide the mark given to a response. These key words and the criteria for each band can be found in the table below.

Band	Marks	Key words/phrases	Explanation
1	1–2 marks	'identify', 'begin to comment'	This means that you are beginning to find some relevant details and, in some cases, can make simple points about them.
2	3–4 marks	'straightforward'	This means that you can find some relevant details and make simple but clear points about them.
3	5–6 marks	'some understanding'	This means that you show some awareness of the writer's intended meaning and can give reasons to support your examples.
4	7–8 marks	'accurate', 'begin to analyse'	This means that you have given a range of precise points and are able to examine the evidence carefully.
5	9–10 marks	'perceptive', 'wide range', 'detailed analysis'	This means that you have made a wide range of observant and insightful points and are able to examine the evidence carefully and thoroughly.

Tip

You may be asked to comment on structure as part of your response to either Question 2, 3 or 4 in the Component 1 exam. The bullet points and italicised text that follow the exam question may indicate whether or not you are expected to analyse structure as part of your answer, so it's important to read the question text carefully.

Understanding the mark scheme

Mark scheme

Below is the mark scheme for the sample Question 3 from the practice paper. The key words from each band have been highlighted to help you see how the skills level increases, as progress is made through the bands.

Band 1	Give 1–2 marks to those who **identify** and **begin to comment** on some examples of the Oxenford family's reactions.
Band 2	Give 3–4 marks to those who identify and give **straightforward** comments on some examples of the Oxenford family's reactions. These examples may identify some relevant subject terminology.
Band 3	Give 5–6 marks to those who identify and comment on a number of different examples of the Oxenford family's reactions and begin to show **some understanding** of how aspects such as language and organisation are used to achieve effects and influence the reader. These responses may begin to use relevant subject terminology accurately to support their comments, where appropriate.
Band 4	Give 7–8 marks to those who make **accurate** comments about a range of different examples of the Oxenford family's reactions and **begin to analyse** how language and the organisation of events are used to achieve effects and influence the reader. Relevant subject terminology is used accurately to support comments effectively, where appropriate.
Band 5	Give 9–10 marks to those who make accurate and **perceptive** comments about a **wide range** of different examples of the Oxenford family's reactions and provide **detailed analysis** of how language and the organisation of events are used to achieve effects and influence the reader. Subtleties of the writer's technique are explored in relation to how the reader is influenced. Well-considered, accurate use of relevant subject terminology supports comments effectively, where appropriate.

The mark scheme also includes a list of indicative content. This provides suggested examples of the content that you may include as part of a successful answer to Question 3. This is not a complete list, but is a good indicator of the most relevant content for the answer. Below is the indicative content list for the sample Question 3.

Details candidates may explore or comment on could be:

- the reader's expectation that Margaret will react positively: she has 'read with fascination' about the benefits for women from the 'last war'/'dreamed of volunteering'
- the family's normal routine is not interrupted to hear the news of the war
- Margaret feels fierce excitement: 'savage glee'
- Margaret's father does not react: he 'said grace' and continues as normal
- 'Bates offered Mother the smoked salmon', for Margaret's parents, the meal continues as though nothing has happened
- Margaret's mother points out 'there's only one thing to be done' as if it were obvious
- Margaret's mother engages with the topic in an 'offhand tone', suggesting she is not concerned
- Margaret is outraged: 'No!'/'horrified'/'burst out'
- Margaret's mother's plan is introduced without room for discussion: 'We must all go and live in America'
- the war seems something Margaret's mother has no feelings for, beyond the inconvenience it will cause: 'silly war'
- dialogue is repressed – her mother more concerned with 'peace and harmony' of lunch
- Margaret repeats herself but her 'outrage' renders her 'almost speechless'
- Margaret seems young: 'It's not fair!'/has to 'choke down a sob'
- Margaret's passion contrasts with her parents' apparent calmness/ambivalence
- day-to-day activities are used to emphasise her parent's business-as-usual approach

This is not a checklist and the question must be marked in levels of response. Look for and reward valid alternatives.

Chapter 2: Component 1

Sample student responses

Below are extracts from two different answers to this question. The first extract is taken from an answer that was given a mark in Band 2 and the second extract is taken from an answer that was given a mark in Band 4.

Student A

Margaret is pleased they are now at war because she 'has dreamed of volunteering'. The word 'dreamed' shows she has thought about it a lot. Her reaction is also excited as she feels 'glee' which suggests she is excited. A simile is also used to show she felt excitement 'like the excitement of driving too fast'. Margaret's parents did not seem bothered and thought the war was 'silly' and that they should 'go and live in America' until it was over. They just want to have their lunch in 'peace and harmony'.

Student B

We expect Margaret to be positive about the news of war because it will allow her to achieve some of her ambitions. She has 'dreamed of volunteering' for the women's army, which suggests this is something she has thought about with hope for the future. When the news comes, she feels 'savage glee', which shows she is really excited and we get the sense, especially with the word 'savage', that this is in a wild way, and that her feelings take over her. The writer uses a simile to compare this excitement as being 'like the excitement of driving too fast', which again makes it seem like an adrenalin rush or that she is overtaken by her feelings. The writing is organised to emphasise the difference between Margaret's reaction and that of her family. Whilst she is clearly experiencing excitement her father's reaction is in complete contrast as he continues as normal, he 'said grace and they sat down' ready to continue with an ordinary Sunday lunch.

Activity 5 Building levels of response

1. Look at the two sample answers. Student A was awarded a Band 2 mark for the answer and Student B's answer is part of a Band 4 response. What do you think the differences are between these two answers? Complete the following steps:

    a. Underline any reactions given in these answers.
    b. Tick where supporting evidence has been used correctly.
    c. Highlight any words or phrases that show analysis.
    d. Circle where subject terminology supports the comments made effectively.

2. Look at the indicative content on page 53. One of the points made is that dialogue is used to show the family's reactions.

    a. Identify a couple of pieces of evidence that show that the writer's use of dialogue is key to revealing the different reactions of the Oxenford family.
    b. Write two to three sentences, using the evidence you have selected, to show how dialogue is used to reveal the different reactions of the Oxenford family.

> c. Now review the sentences you have written. Annotate your writing to indicate where you have referred to the question, where you have used evidence from the text, where you have explained your point and where you have used any relevant subject terminology.

Improving your Section A: Question 3 response

Activity 6 Self-assessment

1. Now look at your original response to this question. Compare it to the examples given for Band 2 and Band 4 answers and then use the mark scheme and indicative content on page 53 to decide which band your response fits into.

2. Think about how you could improve your response. Look particularly at the way you have used and analysed the evidence from the text:

    a. Does the evidence you have selected fit the point you are making?
    b. Have you analysed the evidence?
    c. Have you shown clear understanding of how the language and organisation of the text is used to achieve effects and influence the reader?
    d. Have you tracked carefully through the text and found a decent range of points?
    e. Have you used relevant subject terminology to further demonstrate your understanding?
    f. Have you considered the advice given in the Upgrade panel?

3. Rewrite your response, paying particular attention to the areas you have identified above that could be developed or improved. Check your revised answer against the mark scheme to see if it would now achieve a higher mark.

Upgrade

- Remember to track through the text – reading the text in chronological order will aid your awareness of the way the writing is sequenced and add to your understanding of structure.
- Think about the possible reasons behind the writer's structural choices and release of information, for example, the emphasis on normal day-to-day activities and the variation of sentence structure.
- It's important to remember the writer makes carefully selected language choices to reveal different things about different members of the family. For example, Margaret's mother sometimes sounds as though she is speaking to very young children. How do words and phrases such as 'silly war' and 'squabbling' help to emphasise that?

Chapter 2: Component 1

Section A: Question 4

Read the sample Question 4 below from the practice exam paper on pages 38–41.

Example Exam Question

> | 0 | 4 | Read lines 48–75.
>
> What are Margaret's thoughts and feelings in these lines? How does the writer show her thoughts and feelings?
>
> You should write about:
> - what happens in these lines
> - the writer's use of language
>
> **[10 marks]**
>
> *You must refer to the language used in the text to support your answer, using relevant subject terminology where appropriate.*

This question tests your ability to explain, comment on and analyse how writers use language to achieve effects and influence readers, using relevant subject terminology where appropriate (AO2 1a, c and d).

Question 4 is assessed using marking bands: each band contains key words and phrases, which examiners use to decide the mark given to a response. These key words and the criteria for each band can be found in the table below.

Band	Marks	Key words/phrases	Explanation
1	1–2 marks	'identify', 'straightforward feelings'	This means that you can locate and present some of Margaret's more obvious thoughts and feelings.
2	3–4 marks	'identify', 'some understanding'	This means that you can find some of Margaret's thoughts and feelings and make points about them which show some awareness of the writer's meaning.
3	5–6 marks	'a range', 'begin to analyse'	This means you show awareness of the writer's intended meaning and are starting to examine the evidence. You can do this over a range of examples.
4	7–8 marks	'range', 'detailed analysis'	This means that you have given a range of precise thoughts and feelings and are able to examine the evidence that led you to these points carefully.
5	9–10 marks	'accurate and perceptive', 'subtleties of writer's technique'	This means that you have made a wide range of observant and insightful points about Margaret's thoughts and feelings. You are able to examine the evidence carefully and thoroughly and distinguish between layers of meaning.

Understanding the mark scheme

Mark scheme

Below is the mark scheme for the sample Question 4 from the practice paper. The key words from each band have been highlighted to help you see how the skills level increases, as progress is made through the bands.

Band 1	Give 1–2 marks to those who **identify** some **straightforward feelings** of Margaret. Subject terminology may be used.
Band 2	Give 3–4 marks to those who **identify** some of Margaret's thoughts and feelings and begin to show **some understanding** of how language is used to achieve effects and influence the reader. These responses may identify some subject terminology, where appropriate.
Band 3	Give 5–6 marks to those who give **a range** of Margaret's thoughts and feelings and **begin to analyse** how language is used to achieve effects and influence the reader. These answers may use relevant subject terminology, where appropriate.
Band 4	Give 7–8 marks to those who give a **range** of Margaret's thoughts and feelings and provide **detailed analysis** of how language is used to achieve effects and influence the reader. Subject terminology is used accurately, where appropriate.
Band 5	Give 9–10 marks to those who make **accurate and perceptive** comments about Margaret's thoughts and feelings and provide detailed analysis of how language is used to achieve effects and influence the reader. **Subtleties of the writer's technique** are explored in relation to how the reader is influenced. Well-considered, accurate use of relevant subject terminology supports comments effectively, where appropriate.

The mark scheme also includes a list of indicative content. This provides suggested examples of the content that you may include as part of a successful answer to Question 4. This is not a complete list, but is a good indicator of the most relevant content for the answer. Below is the indicative content list for the sample Question 4.

Details candidates may explore or comment on could be:

- she feels 'unable to eat'
- she 'drank endless cups of tea' while servants pack up the house
- it is clear she 'was not going to pack'
- Margaret feels sorry for Jenkins' 'bad luck'
- she listens with interest to Jenkins' plans
- she is 'startled' by the news that 'there's nothing your parents can do' once someone of 18 has signed on
- she answers 'thoughtfully' when she admits she didn't know
- she realises she must do 'something other than sulk'
- she resolves to 'confront her father'
- she feels 'shaky' at the thought
- she thinks carefully about what she should say and how she should behave
- she knows she must 'appear sensible, responsible, mature'
- she thinks through her points: 'live with relatives'/'no reason why she should not'
- she convinces herself that she is an adult – list of things that 19-year-olds do
- she reassures herself: 'That made sense'
- she gathers her 'courage'
- use of omniscient narrator to convey her distraction and her thought processes

This is not a checklist and the question must be marked in levels of response. Look for and reward valid alternatives.

Chapter 2: Component 1

Sample student responses

Below are extracts from two different answers to this question. The first extract is taken from an answer that was given a mark in Band 3 and the second extract is taken from an answer that was given a mark in Band 5.

Student A

Margaret felt 'unable to eat' and 'she drank endless cups of tea'. This presents the idea that she was anxious and did not quite know what to do with herself. She could not bring herself to pack but she feels sorry for Jenkins who has only just started work with them and now they have 'decided to close up the house'. Margaret begins to realise that things aren't quite as she thought though as Jenkins is adamant 'there'll be no shortage of work'. This is added to when she is 'startled' that parents can't do anything to stop you if you've joined the war.

Student B

The writer demonstrates Margaret's feelings of anxiety and distress by describing her as 'unable to eat' and drinking 'endless cups of tea', like a compulsive action. This implies she is doing this to soothe her nerves or as a form of distraction. Despite this, Margaret still feels sympathy for Jenkins, even though she had only been working with them for a week. Her friendly dialogue with Jenkins is conveyed, as she describes it as 'bad luck' that Jenkins would now be out of a job. This dialogue also gives the reader an awareness of Margaret's inexperience of the world as Jenkins is worldlier. Their conversation furthers Margaret's awareness of the law around signing on and she is 'startled' by the knowledge that an eighteen-year-old can sign on without parents being able to intervene. Her question of 'Are you sure?' shows her interest and gives the sense that the news will jolt her out of her previous feelings of anxiety and towards taking some action for herself.

> ### ✏️ Activity 7 Building levels of response
>
> 1. Look at the two sample answers. Student A was awarded a Band 3 mark for the answer and Student B's answer is part of a Band 5 response. What do you think the differences are between these two answers? Complete the following steps:
>   a. Underline any thoughts and feelings given in these answers.
>   b. Tick where evidence has been used to support the answer.
>   c. Highlight any comments that you think are perceptive.
>   d. Circle all the points made and decide if a range of different points is covered.
>
> 2. Look again at the list of indicative content on page 57. There are a number of points about how Margaret thinks she will have to behave when she speaks to her father.
>   a. Select two or three pieces of evidence you could use to show her thoughts and feelings about this.
>   b. Write down two or three sentences to analyse the writer's language in this evidence.
>   c. Review the sentences you have written. Annotate your writing to indicate where you have referred to the question, where you have used evidence from the text, where you have analysed language and where you have used relevant subject terminology.

Understanding the mark scheme

Improving your Section A: Question 4 response

Activity 8 Self-assessment

1. Now look again at your original response to this question. Compare it to the Band 3 and Band 5 answers and then use the mark scheme and indicative content on page 57 to decide which band your response fits into.

2. Think about how you could improve your response. Look particularly at the way you have used and analysed evidence from the text:

   a. Does the evidence you have selected fit the point you are making?
   b. Have you written about Margaret's thoughts and feelings?
   c. Have you analysed the evidence clearly?
   d. Have you shown clear understanding of how the writer's language is used to achieve effects and influence the reader?
   e. Have you used relevant subject terminology to further demonstrate your understanding? For example, a **metaphor** is used when Margaret is described as going back to her room to 'steel her nerves'.
   f. Have you explained the effects of these devices?

3. Rewrite your response, paying particular attention to the areas you have identified above that could be developed or improved. Check your revised answer against the mark scheme to see if it would now achieve a higher mark.

Upgrade

- Remember to track through the text – reading the text in chronological order will aid your awareness of Margaret's thoughts and feelings and any changes to them.
- Always consider the reasons behind the writer's choices; they will be for a deliberate effect. For example, look at the words 'shaky' and 'nerves'. Both suggest Margaret is fearful of something: she does not want to 'enrage' her father. What does this language imply about their relationship?

Key term

metaphor: when a thing or person is described as something else for dramatic effect e.g. 'the market was a hive of activity'.

59

Chapter 2: Component 1

Section A: Question 5

Read the sample Question 5 below from the practice exam paper on pages 38–41.

Example Exam Question

> **0 5** To answer this question you need to read lines 76-84 and also consider the passage as whole.
>
> 'The writer presents Margaret as someone who has no choice but to act on impulse.'
>
> How far do you agree with this view?
>
> You should write about:
>
> - your thoughts and feelings about how Margaret is presented in the passage as a whole
> - how the writer has created these thoughts and feelings
>
> [10 marks]
>
> *You must refer to the text to support your answer.*

This question tests your ability to evaluate texts critically and support this with appropriate textual reference (AO4). Question 5 is assessed using marking bands: each band contains key words and phrases, which examiners use to decide the mark given to a response. These key words and the criteria for each band can be found in the table below.

Band	Marks	Key words/phrases	Explanation
1	1–2 marks	'simple personal opinion', 'linked, basic textual reference'	This means that you can offer a simple view in relation to the character of Margaret and the statement in the question and can link this to evidence from the text.
2	3–4 marks	'personal opinion', 'straightforward textual references'	This means that you give clear views in relation to the character of Margaret and the statement in the question and are able to support these views with evidence from the text.
3	5–6 marks	'evaluation', 'some critical awareness'	This means that you can express your views and make judgements based on what you have read. You use evidence to support your views. You show some ability to analyse how the evidence has influenced you with regard to Margaret's character and are beginning to show an overview of the whole text.
4	7–8 marks	'critical evaluation', 'critical awareness', 'well-selected textual references'	This means that you can express your views and make judgements in an analytical way. You use carefully chosen evidence to support your views about the presentation of Margaret's character and are clearly engaged with specific detail as well as the whole text.
5	9–10 marks	'persuasive evaluation', 'convincing, well-selected examples', 'purposeful textual references', 'overview'	This means that you can express convincing views and make judgements in an analytical and insightful way. You use carefully chosen evidence to support your views and are fully engaged by the text. You are able to offer detailed analysis of specific evidence as well as stand back and write about the presentation of character as a whole.

Understanding the mark scheme

Mark scheme

Below is the mark scheme for the sample Question 5 from the practice paper. The key words from each band have been highlighted to help you see how the skills level increases, as progress is made through the bands.

Band 1	Give 1–2 marks to those who express a simple personal opinion with linked, basic textual reference.
Band 2	Give 3–4 marks to those who give a personal opinion supported by straightforward textual references. These responses will show limited interaction with the text as a whole and/or how the writer has created the reader's thoughts and feelings.
Band 3	Give 5–6 marks to those who give an evaluation of the text and its effects, supported by appropriate textual references. These responses will show some critical awareness of the text as a whole and how the writer has created the reader's thoughts and feelings.
Band 4	Give 7–8 marks to those who give a critical evaluation of the text and its effects, supported by well-selected textual references. These responses will show critical awareness and clear engagement with the text. They will also explore how the writer has created the reader's thoughts and feelings.
Band 5	Give 9–10 marks to those who give a persuasive evaluation of the text and its effects, supported by convincing, well-selected examples and purposeful textual references. These responses will show engagement and involvement, where candidates take an overview to make accurate and perceptive comments on the text as a whole. They will also explore how the writer has created the reader's thoughts and feelings with insight.

The mark scheme also includes a list of indicative content. This provides suggested examples of the content that you may include as part of a successful answer to Question 5. This is not a complete list, but is a good indicator of the most relevant content for the answer. Below is the indicative content list for the sample Question 5.

Areas for possible evaluation could be:

- **initially we get the sense that Margaret is not in control of her own life**
- she was 'fuming' because she was 'forced' to attend church by her father
- her boredom is evident – even the church bell 'tolled a monotonous note'
- **there is little expectation of her ever being able to decide for herself**
- her mother thinks future decisions will be 'up to your husband' and her father treats her like a child: 'Don't be ridiculous'
- **she is a person of strong opinions and feelings and feels trapped by her life**
- she 'dreaded war' and the 'grief' she knew, yet also wants war to feel proud of her country
- she wants an end to the 'narrow, suffocating life' with her parents
- she dreams of 'volunteering'
- she has some skills she wants to use: 'she could drive'/'she could even handle a motor boat'
- **Margaret is emotionally charged by the news they are at war**
- she feels 'savage glee'
- she thinks all of the awful things connected with war are now unavoidable and 'the only thing to do was fight'
- **her parents and the meal continue as normal**
- her mother refers to it as a 'silly war' as if it's just an inconvenience, and struggles to communicate her arguments
- **Margaret works through the sensible arguments to tackle her father**
- she thinks/hopes all she needs is 'courage'
- evidence of the rest of the text suggests her arguments will come to nothing
- **she comes up with an escape plan quickly and on impulse**
- this way 'it would be too late' for her parents to stop her

This is not a checklist and the question must be marked in levels of response. Look for and reward valid alternatives.

Chapter 2: Component 1

Sample student responses

Below are extracts from two different answers to this question. The first extract is taken from an answer that was given a mark in Band 2 and the second extract is taken from an answer that was given a mark in Band 4.

Student A

I agree with this statement as Margaret can't seem to do anything or even speak unless she agrees with her parents. At the start she 'fuming because she was forced to go to church' and even though she has said she doesn't want to go she still does because 'as far as they were concerned the argument was over' and she has to do what her parents say. Even after they are at war her parents carry on as if nothing has happened and her mum even calls it a 'silly war'. If she wants to get away she will have to act quickly because they won't listen to her.

Student B

I agree to some extent with this statement as Margaret is presented as someone who is trapped by the life she is living. It is clear that she lacks control over her own life despite her having fairly strong opinions. We know that she is 'fuming' because she was 'forced' to attend church. The word 'fuming' suggests the extent of her anger with 'forced' making it clear that she is attending against her will. The extent to which she is trapped is made clear by the fact that she has tried to put across her own opinion but appears to be treated like a child in these situations. Her father tells her 'Don't be ridiculous' when she questions whether she needs to go to church which suggests that he doesn't listen to what she has to say.

Activity 9 Building levels of response

1. Look at the two sample answers. Student A was awarded a Band 2 mark for the answer and Student B's answer is part of a Band 4 response. What do you think the differences are between these two answers? Complete the following steps:

   a. Underline any examples of personal opinion.
   b. Circle any examples of critical evaluation.
   c. Tick where evidence has been included.
   d. Highlight where evidence has been analysed and note how this is different in each answer.

2. Look at the list of indicative content on page 61. The first bullet point is emboldened. This is because it is an overview point and some of the following points can be linked to it.

   a. Choose at least two points from the indicative content that you would use to support this overview point.

Understanding the mark scheme

b. Write two or three sentences to analyse your selected evidence and evaluate how this presents Margaret as someone who has no choice but to act on impulse.

c. Review the sentences you have written. Annotate your writing to show where you have used evidence from the text, where you have analysed the evidence and where you have addressed the question and evaluated how Margaret is presented.

Improving your Section A: Question 5 response

Activity 10 Self-assessment

1. Now look again at your original response to Question 5. Compare it to the Band 2 and Band 4 answers and then use the mark scheme and indicative content on page 61 to decide which band your response fits into.

2. Think about how you could improve your response:

    a. Have you tracked through the text carefully and found a range of points?
    b. Have you explored your thoughts and feelings about Margaret?
    c. Have you considered how the writer influences your feelings?
    d. Have you found a clear range of evidence and used it to support your agreement or disagreement with the statement in the question?
    e. Have you considered the points in the upgrade panel?

3. Rewrite your response, paying particular attention to the areas you have identified above that could be developed or improved. Check your revised answer against the mark scheme to see if it would now achieve a higher mark.

Upgrade

- Remember to track through the whole text – reading the text in chronological order will aid the coherence of your answer. You must show clarity in your ideas about the way Margaret is presented.
- Focus on what the writer has done to influence your opinions. Look carefully at the writer's language choices and methods. Your opinions about Margaret have been influenced by the way the writer has put this text together – try to show how your views have been formed.
- Consider whether you can make any overview points of how Margaret is presented. Drawing together multiple points of evidence in support of a general line of argument will demonstrate your ability to stand back from the text and write about the presentation of the character as a whole.

Chapter 2: Component 1

Section B: Question 1

Read the sample Question 1 below from Section B of the practice exam paper on pages 38–41.

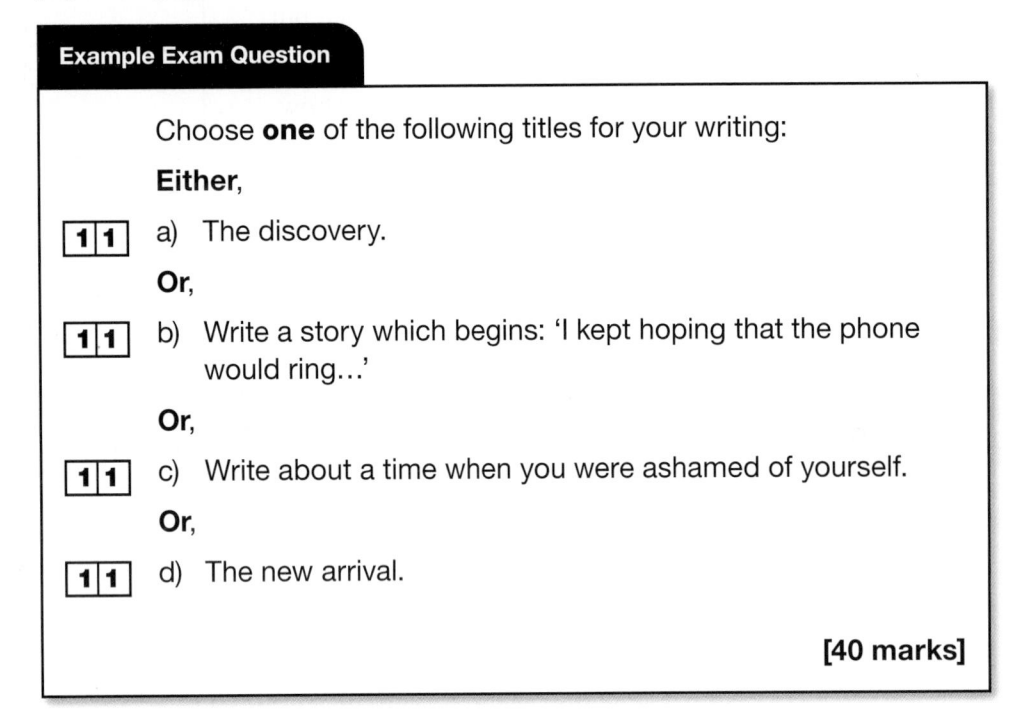

> **Example Exam Question**
>
> Choose **one** of the following titles for your writing:
>
> **Either,**
>
> 1 1   a)   The discovery.
>
> Or,
>
> 1 1   b)   Write a story which begins: 'I kept hoping that the phone would ring...'
>
> Or,
>
> 1 1   c)   Write about a time when you were ashamed of yourself.
>
> Or,
>
> 1 1   d)   The new arrival.
>
>   **[40 marks]**

This question tests your ability to communicate your ideas and organise a text effectively (AO5). You need to be able to:

- communicate clearly, effectively and imaginatively, selecting and adapting tone, style and register for different forms, purposes and audiences
- organise information and ideas, using structural and grammatical features to support coherence and cohesion of texts.

This question also tests the accuracy of your vocabulary, sentence structure, spelling and punctuation (AO6). You need to be able to:

- use a range of vocabulary and sentence structures for clarity, purpose and effect, with accurate spelling and punctuation.

Question 1 in Section B of the Component 1 exam paper is worth 40 marks.

The mark scheme is divided into two sections to reflect the two assessment objectives. Of the 40 marks available, the quality of your communication and organisation (AO5) is worth 24 marks, and the quality of your vocabulary, sentence structure, spelling and punctuation (AO6) is worth 16 marks.

Communication and Organisation (AO5)

The mark scheme for Communication and Organisation (AO5) is divided into marking bands: each band contains key words and phrases, which examiners use to decide the mark given to a response. These key words and the criteria for each band can be found in the table below.

Band	Key words/phrases	Explanation
1	'basic control and coherence', 'basic organisation', 'communication is limited'	This means that your writing is quite simple and is not always organised in a way that makes sense. You may make some points clearly. Your reader struggles to follow what you have written.
2	'some control and coherence', 'some organisation', 'communication is limited but clear'	This means that your writing is sometimes clear and sometimes makes sense. Your writing is sometimes organised and some ideas make sense and you try to develop them sensibly. You have tried to be clear in the way you put across your ideas but may not always be successful. Sometimes the reader may struggle to understand or lose the sense of what you were trying to say.
3	'mostly controlled and coherent', 'shape and direction', 'communication is clear but limited in ambition'	This means that your writing is mostly clear and mostly makes sense as a whole. You can organise your writing with a sense of purpose and you are generally able to make your meaning clear. Your work may be quite straightforward and not demonstrate the careful crafting of a higher band, but your reader will be able to understand your meaning.
4	'clearly controlled and coherent', 'convincing detail', 'clearly organised', 'some ambition', 'precise meaning'	This means that your writing is clear and makes sense as a whole. You can organise your writing with clarity and you use language carefully to communicate your ideas. Your ideas are consistent, effectively developed and relevant to the task. Your reader is interested by what you write.
5	'fully coherent', 'developed with originality', 'sophisticated', 'fully engages', 'ambitious', 'consistently conveys precise meaning'	This means that your writing has been crafted with confidence and ambition. You know how to structure writing accurately and are willing to be imaginative and sophisticated in your use of language and ideas. You are able to fully engage your reader and make sure that they are emotionally involved in the narrative.

Below, and on page 66, is the mark scheme for Communication and Organisation (AO5) for Section B: Question 1 of the practice paper on pages 38–41. The key words from each band have been highlighted to help you see how the skills level increases, as progress is made through the bands.

Band 1	**1–4 marks** • there is basic control and coherence (a basic sense of plot and characterisation) • there is basic organisation (paragraphs may be used to show obvious divisions) • there is some use of structure and grammatical features to convey meaning • communication is limited but some meaning is conveyed
Band 2	**5–9 marks** • there is some control and coherence (some control of plot and characterisation) • there is some organisation (narrative is beginning to have some shape and development) • structure and grammatical features are used to convey meaning • communication is limited but clear
Band 3	**10–14 marks** • the writing is mostly controlled and coherent (plot and characterisation show some detail and development) • the writing is organised (narrative has shape and direction) • structure and grammatical features are used with some accuracy to convey meaning • communication is clear but limited in ambition

Chapter 2: Component 1

Band 4	**15–19 marks** • the writing is clearly controlled and coherent (plot and characterisation show convincing detail and some originality and imagination) • the writing is clearly organised (narrative is purposefully shaped and developed) • structure and grammatical features are used accurately to support cohesion and coherence • communication shows some ambition and conveys precise meaning
Band 5	**20–24 marks** • the writing is fully coherent and controlled (plot and characterisation are developed with detail, originality and imagination) • the writing is clearly and imaginatively organised (narrative is sophisticated and fully engages the reader's interest) • structure and grammatical features are used ambitiously to give the writing cohesion and coherence • communication is ambitious and consistently conveys precise meaning

Vocabulary, Sentence structure, Spelling and Punctuation (AO6)

The mark scheme for Vocabulary, Sentence structure, Spelling and Punctuation (AO6) is also divided into five marking bands: each band contains key words and phrases, which examiners use to decide the mark given to a response. These key words and the criteria for each band can be found in the table below.

Band	Key words/phrases	Explanation
1	'limited range', 'limited control', 'some attempt to use…'	This means that your writing is not very accurate. Your spelling and use of punctuation and grammar contain basic errors that hinder the meaning and/or your sentences lack variety. If you were to underline all of the errors in your work there would probably be a lot of areas underlined in your writing.
2	'some variety', 'some control', 'usually accurate', 'generally secure', 'some range'	This means that your writing is sometimes accurate. Spelling, punctuation and grammar are sometimes controlled but there will be some errors across multiple areas (for example, in spelling, punctuation and grammar). Your use of vocabulary shows some range but this may be simple and/or have mixed success.
3	'variety in sentence structure', 'mostly secure', 'mostly accurately', 'beginning to develop'	This means that your writing is mostly accurate and reliable. Spelling, punctuation and grammar are mostly controlled. Your use of vocabulary is beginning to show care and some thought.
4	'varied', 'secure', 'range'	This means that your writing is generally very accurate and reliable. Spelling, punctuation and grammar are accurate and care has been taken. Your use of vocabulary is careful and thoughtful.
5	'appropriate and effective variation', 'controlled and accurate', 'confidently', 'totally secure', 'wide range', 'ambitious'	This means that your writing is extremely accurate. Errors rarely occur and your writing is technically sophisticated and carefully crafted for effect. You can use a wide range of carefully chosen vocabulary for maximum effect.

Understanding the mark scheme

Below is the mark scheme for Vocabulary, Sentence structure, Spelling and Punctuation (AO6) for Section B: Question 1 of the practice paper on pages 38–41. The key words from each band have been highlighted to help you see how the skills level increases, as progress is made through the bands.

Band 1	**1–3 marks** • limited range of sentence structure • limited control of sentence construction • there is some attempt to use punctuation • some spelling is accurate • control of tense and agreement is limited • limited range of vocabulary
Band 2	**4–6 marks** • some variety of sentence structure • there is some control of sentence construction • some control of a range of punctuation • the spelling is usually accurate • control of tense and agreement is generally secure • there is some range of vocabulary
Band 3	**7–10 marks** • there is variety in sentence structure • control of sentence construction is mostly secure • a range of punctuation is used, mostly accurately • most spelling, including that of irregular words, is correct • control of tense and agreement is mostly secure • vocabulary is beginning to develop and is used with some precision
Band 4	**11–13 marks** • sentence structure is varied to achieve particular effects • control of sentence construction is secure • a range of punctuation is used accurately • spelling, including that of irregular words, is secure • control of tense and agreement is secure • vocabulary is ambitious and used with precision
Band 5	**14–16 marks** • there is appropriate and effective variation of sentence structures • virtually all sentence construction is controlled and accurate • a range of punctuation is used confidently and accurately • virtually all spelling, including that of complex irregular words, is correct • control of tense and agreement is totally secure • a wide range of appropriate, ambitious vocabulary is used to create effect or convey precise meaning

Improving your Section B: Question 1 response

Activity 11 Self-assessment

1. Now read your original response to Section B: Question 1. Refer back to the mark scheme for Communication and Organisation (AO5) on pages 65–66. Decide which mark your response would be given.

2. Think about how you could improve your response. Consider the points below:

   Organisation:
   - Did you write a plan to help you organise your thinking and work out the sequencing of your narrative?
   - Is your plot coherent and are characters developed convincingly?
   - Have you linked your ideas convincingly?
   - Have you paragraphed your writing effectively?
   - Is your writing relevant to the task?

   Communication
   - Have you written in sufficient detail?
   - Have you worked to engage your reader? For example, through the use of questions, humour or even comments directed specifically to the reader.
   - Have you thought carefully about vocabulary and how you could use linguistic devices?
   - If you were instructed to write with a particular ending or beginning in mind have you achieved this?

3. Now refer to the mark scheme for Vocabulary, Sentence structure, Spelling and Punctuation (AO6) on page 67. Review each sentence of your writing, and decide which mark your response would be given for this mark scheme.

4. Think about how your technical accuracy could be improved. Read your writing in detail and check the following:

   a. Have you made any frequent spelling errors?
   b. Have you copied down all spellings accurately from the exam paper?
   c. Have you used a range of different punctuation types, for example, full stops, questions marks and commas?

Understanding the mark scheme

    d. Have you used tenses and verb agreement correctly in your writing?

    e. Have you varied the length and order of your sentences?

5. Rewrite your response, paying particular attention to the areas you have identified above that could be developed or improved, as well as the Upgrade advice that is printed below. Check your revised answer against the mark schemes to see if it would now achieve a higher mark.

Upgrade

- Think carefully about the plot of your writing, including the way that you sequence events. Are you going to include an interesting opening or ending? How could you create an immediate atmosphere or build the narrative to a point of tension? Could you include plot devices, like dialogue or flashbacks?
- Consider how you want your story to be read; give your reader a clear perspective (using first person or third person) or use an omniscient narrator to give the reader an insight.
- Take the time to add colour and interest to your story through the setting and mood and closely-observed detail that will capture your reader's interest.
- Make decisions about the key characters in the story, and focus on their emotions and behaviour to achieve effects.
- Plan your writing thoroughly. A plan will help you to think through all of these elements and make sure that your ideas are well organised before you begin to write.
- Remember you want your reader to understand what you are writing. Check your writing for spelling, punctuation and grammar, as well as use of the correct tense, which can often cause meaning to break down. If you start writing in one tense, use it consistently throughout your writing.

Chapter 2: Component 1

Component 1: Progress check

Now you have looked at both of the Component 1 practice papers in detail, you can review which questions you feel confident about and where you think there are improvements to be made. Look back at the 'What you have to do' lists in the 'Preparing to practise' sections of Chapter 1 and Chapter 2. These will remind you of the skills you need to demonstrate in each question.

Then, complete the following progress check.

	I am confident in this skill	I have some confidence in this skill	I need more practice in this skill
Section A			
Question 1			
I can find five things in the set lines about the set focus.			
Question 2			
I can write down different impressions and use evidence to support my answer.			
I can write about how the selected evidence helped to create the impression.			
I can analyse the effects of the selected evidence.			
Question 3			
I can keep a clear focus on the question.			
I can choose evidence carefully and with the question in mind.			
I can analyse the way language is used.			
I can write about the effects of structure.			
I can use subject terminology when relevant to support my answer.			
Question 4			
I can keep a clear focus on the question.			
I can write a range of ideas in relation to the question.			
I can analyse the way language is used.			
I can use subject terminology when relevant to support my answer.			
Question 5			
I can consider the text as a whole.			
I can consider my own thoughts and feelings about the character and how she is presented.			
I can support my evaluation with relevant textual references.			
I can focus on the statement given in the question.			

Component 1: Progress check

	I am confident in this skill	I have some confidence in this skill	I need more practice in this skill
Section B			
Question 1			
I can choose from a series of writing titles.			
I can plan a piece of narrative writing in a way that helps me.			
I can produce a piece of narrative writing that engages a reader.			
I can communicate clearly.			
I can adapt my tone and style to the task set.			
I can develop detail convincingly.			
I can use carefully chosen vocabulary.			
I can use linguistic devices to enhance my writing.			
I can structure and organise my writing effectively.			
I can spell accurately.			
I can use punctuation accurately.			
I can use grammar accurately.			
I can vary my sentences effectively.			
I can use punctuation effectively.			
I can use grammar effectively.			
I can use tenses accurately and consistently.			
I can proofread my own writing.			

Chapter 3: Component 2

Component 2 sample exam paper

The following account has been taken from Leah Davis' blog about her day out in Camden Market.

Camden Market: My Favorite Day Out in London

As I often do on my travels, I went to London having done very little research. I like to let my trips happen organically and to leave myself open to suggestions by friends or locals. When Camden Market was given to me as a suggestion for how to spend the day, I didn't think twice – nor did I check it out on the interwebs before arriving. Instead, I simply hopped on a bus with camera in hand, more or less oblivious to what I was about to find. I do love a good surprise, and Camden Market wasn't just a good one, it was *amazing*.

I exited the bus at Camden High Street near the Camden Town underground. […] The shops on Camden High Street are a sight to behold in their own right. The storefronts are either brightly painted or elaborately decorated with sculptures representing the goods they sell; the crowd hanging around seemed a bit on the young side, so I felt right at home (har, har). I wandered past pubs, kitschy tourist shops, and fruit juice stands. I was already experiencing serious sensory overload and little did I know that this was just the tip of the iceberg.

Making my way further north, I eventually encountered Camden Lock, the gateway to the elaborate labyrinth of shops that compose Camden Market. I still hadn't made any purchases but my belly was starting to rumble, so I wandered in hoping to stumble upon the food court. I had purposely waited to eat lunch because street food was the one thing I knew for certain I'd find at Camden Market that day. It didn't take long for the scents of a million different delicacies to hit my nose. I bobbed and weaved through a few beautiful market halls, trusting my schnoz to lead me to paradise.

The food court at Camden Market turned out to be one of my favorite places I ate that week; my only regret was not having a hollow leg or two so I could've tried more, more, more! Peruvian, Malaysian, Korean, French, Venezuelan, Turkish – the appropriately named Global Kitchen had just about every corner of the globe represented. There were healthy options and plenty of vegetarian and vegan choices, too. There was something for everyone, and for bargain prices (around £5 for most dishes, £1 for a soda or water). There were plenty of tables (covered, in case it rains, I imagine) so I nabbed a seat beside some friendly strangers and snarfed down my chosen fare, a Turkish wrap filled with chicken and veggies. On my way out, I couldn't help bellying up to another vendor, this time a stall selling Brazilian sweets known as brigadeiros. They are truffle-like confections made of little more than butter, condensed milk and sugar, and I just couldn't resist. […]

I still had a lot of walking to do and was grateful for the extra energy. Next, I was off to explore the rest of the market, divided into sections like North Yard, Middle Yard, and Stables Market. It feels almost as if you're wandering through a secret underground tunnel system; as the names suggest, this part of Camden is the former home of an historic stable and horse hospital. It once housed a sizeable herd that was used to transport goods along the Camden canal. The shops contained within are varied and wacky, with plenty of shiny things vying for your attention and a new surprise hiding around every corner […]

When I make it back to London for another visit, I plan to head straight back to Camden Market. Even if I never plan to buy anything (other than food, of course) there is so much to see, not to mention some top-notch people watching. The melting pot that is London left me captivated, to say the least, and it has Camden Market in large part to thank for that.

In the 19th century there was an extensive general market for butchers' meat and provisions in a section of Somers Town, called the Brill. In this extract from 'London Labour and the London Poor', Henry Mayhew describes a Sunday market at the Brill.

Henry Mayhew's London Markets

As you enter the Brill the market sounds are scarcely heard. But at each step the low hum grows gradually into the noisy shouting, until at last the different cries become distinct, and the hubbub, din, and confusion of a thousand voices bellowing at once fill the air. The road and footpath are crowded, as on the over-night; the men are standing in groups, smoking and talking; whilst the women run to and fro, some with the white round turnips showing out of their filled aprons, others with cabbages under their arms, and a piece of red meat dangling from their hands. Only a few of the shops are closed, but the butcher's and the coal-shed are filled with customers, and from the door of the shut-up baker's the women come streaming forth with bags of flour in their hands, while men sally from the halfpenny barber's smoothing their clean-shaved chins. Walnuts, blacking, apples, onions, braces, combs, turnips, herrings, pens and corn-plaster, are all bellowed out at the same time. Labourers and mechanics, still unshorn and undressed, hang about with their hands in their pockets, some with their pet terriers under their arms. The pavement is green with the refuse leaves of vegetables, and round a cabbage-barrow the women stand turning over the bunches, as the man shouts, 'Where you like, only a penny.' Boys are running home with the breakfast herring held in a piece of paper, and the side-pocket of the apple-man's stuff coat hangs down with the weight of the halfpence stored within it.

Presently the tolling of the neighbouring church bells breaks forth. Then the bustle doubles itself, the cries grow louder, the confusion greater. Women run about and push their way through the throng, scolding the saunterers, for in half an hour the market will close. In a little time the butcher puts up his shutters, and leaves the door still open; the policemen in their clean gloves come round and drive the street-sellers before them, and as the clock strikes eleven the market finishes, and the Sunday's rest begins.

Chapter 3: Component 2

SECTION A: 40 Marks

*Answer **all** the following questions.*

Read the article, 'Camden Market: My Favorite Day Out in London' by Leah Davis.

1 1 a) Where did the writer get off the bus? [1]

b) What is the name of the Brazilian sweet that the writer cannot resist? [1]

c) Which section of the market is Leah Davis' favourite? [1]

1 2 How does the writer try to make Camden Market sound exciting and appealing?

You should comment on:

- what she says
- her use of language, tone and structure
- other ways she tries to make the market sound exciting and appealing [10]

To answer the following questions you will need to read Henry Mayhew's description of the market taken from 'London Labour and the London Poor'.

1 3 a) Name one thing that the women were carrying. [1]

b) How much does it cost for a 'clean-shaved' chin at the barber's? [1]

c) At what time does the market finish? [1]

1 4 'Henry Mayhew presents the market as a busy and chaotic place.' How far do you agree with this view?

You should comment on:

- what he says
- how it is said [10]

You must refer to the text to support your comments.

To answer the following questions you must use both texts.

1 5 Using information from both texts, explain briefly in your own words what attracts visitors to the markets. [4]

1 6 Both of these texts are about London markets.

Compare:

- what the two writers experience during their visit
- how the writers get across their feelings about the markets to their readers [10]

You must use the text to support your comments and make it clear which text you are referring to.

SECTION B: 40 marks

Answer Question 1 and Question 2.

For each question, 12 marks are awarded for communication and organisation; 8 marks are awarded for vocabulary, sentence structure, punctuation and spelling.

Think about the purpose and audience for your writing.

You should aim to write about 300–400 words for each task.

2.1 Write a review for a teenage magazine about the worst book, TV programme or film you have read or watched. Explain why you disliked it and why others should avoid it.

Write your review. [20]

2.2 'Why would anyone visit a shop or market when we can buy everything online?'
You have been asked to give a talk to people in your class giving your views about the above statement.

Write what you would say in your talk. [20]

Chapter 3: Component 2

Preparing to practise

Before you try to complete this practice exam paper, you should think carefully about what skills are being tested in each question and how you can best demonstrate those skills. Read through the following information. It will help you to understand how to answer each question.

Section A: Question 1

Example Exam Question

> **1 1** Read the article, 'Camden Market: My Favorite Day Out in London' by Leah Davis.
>
> a) Where did the writer get off the bus? [1 mark]
>
> b) What is the name of the Brazilian sweet that the writer cannot resist? [1 mark]
>
> c) Which section of the market is Leah Davis' favourite? [1 mark]

You should spend a total of 3–4 minutes on these questions.

What is being tested?

- Your ability to identify **explicit** information. (AO1 1a)

What you have to do

- Identify the correct text.
- Find **specific** details from across the whole passage to answer each of the questions.

Key terms

explicit: stated clearly and openly

specific: detailed and exact, precise

track: read or follow carefully the progress of the text as it develops

chronologically: in the order in which things occurred

Tips

- Check the mark tariff. Each part of Question 1 is usually worth one or two marks, so aim to spend no more than three or four minutes on this question.

- **Track** through the passage **chronologically** – the answer to the first question is likely to appear before the others.

- Use skimming and scanning reading skills to identify the correct area of the text – this will help you to spot topic specific words.

- When you think you have found the answer, read the text surrounding it, to make sure you have the exact piece of information you need.

- Only write down the key details required to answer each question. For example, for Question 1a above, you only need to write the name of a place (where the writer got off the bus).

- Remember to only use information that is explicitly mentioned in the text.

Preparing to practise

Section A: Question 2

Example Exam Question

| 1 2 | How does the writer try to make Camden Market sound exciting and appealing?

You should comment on:
- what she says
- her use of language, tone and structure
- other ways she tries to make the market sound exciting and appealing

[10 marks]

> You should spend about 10–13 minutes on this question.

What is being tested?

- Your ability to explain, comment on and analyse how writers use language and **structure** to achieve effects and influence readers, using relevant subject terminology where appropriate. (AO2 1a, b, c and d)

What you have to do

- Read the whole passage.
- Write down a range of different ways in which the writer makes Camden Market sound appealing and exciting using evidence from the text to support your ideas.
- Think about *how* your chosen ideas/evidence make it sound appealing.
- Where relevant, comment on the effect of the writer's **tone**, style, structure, and language, using relevant subject terminology.

Key terms

structure: the way the text is organised, how it is put together; for example, the writer may use paragraphs, different sentence types and devices such as dialogue deliberately to influence a reader

tone: manner of expression that shows the writer's attitude, e.g. humorous, sarcastic

Tips

- As you write, refer back to the question to make sure you remain on task and link your writing back to the phrasing of the question.
- Remember to explain *how* Camden market is made to sound exciting and appealing in the language, rather than just give examples from the text. Question 2 is assessing how you write about the effects of language.
- Only select evidence that is relevant to the focus of the question.
- Quickly get to the point in your response and remember to be focused in your explanations.
- Track through the text chronologically.
- Do not overlook the importance of language – individual words and phrases can be very effective in making something sound appealing.
- Refer to the bullet points of the question and notice that you must consider the structure of the passage. Does the sequence of the information add to the effect the writer is trying to create?

Chapter 3: Component 2

Section A: Question 3

Example Exam Question

1 3	To answer the following questions you will need to read Henry Mayhew's description of the market taken from 'London Labour and the London Poor'.
	a) Name one thing that the women were carrying. **[1 mark]**
	b) How much does it cost for a 'clean-shaved' chin at the barber's? **[1 mark]**
	c) At what time does the market finish? **[1 mark]**

3-4 minutes — You should only spend about 3–4 minutes on these questions.

What is being tested?

- Your ability to identify and interpret explicit and **implicit** information and ideas. (AO1 1a, b, c and d)

What you have to do

- Look at the instruction above the questions. This tells you that you are now answering questions about a different text.
- Read the questions carefully and identify the correct information in the text.

Tips

- Work through the questions and text chronologically.
- Skim and scan the passage so you are able to find the correct details. Look for the key words from the question and try to find them in the text.
- Always read the sentences surrounding your answer so you can make sure you are reading in **context**.
- Copy down any information from the text carefully to avoid errors.
- Try to answer quickly and efficiently so you can save time for the longer, more demanding questions.
- Label your answers clearly (e.g. 3a, 3b, 3c).
- Remember that Question 3 may assess your skills in finding information that is implied, as well as explicitly stated in the text.

Key terms

implicit: suggested but not directly expressed

context: the words or ideas surrounding something, which can help to clarify the meaning

Preparing to practise

Section A: Question 4

Example Exam Question

| 1 | 4 | 'Henry Mayhew presents the market as a busy and chaotic place.' How far do you agree with this view?

You should comment on:
- what he says
- how it is said

[10 marks]

You must refer to the text to support your comments.

> You should spend about 10–13 minutes on this question.

What is being tested?
- Your ability to **evaluate** texts critically and support this with appropriate textual references. (AO4)

What you have to do
- Read the whole passage and question carefully.
- Look for evidence that conveys the busy and chaotic nature of the market.
- Analyse the effects of your chosen evidence.
- Consider how the writer presents the market in this busy and chaotic way.
- Consider the extent to which you agree with the statement and support your views with details from the text.

Tips

- Remember to carefully read the bullet points that accompany the question. They will tell you exactly what to include in your response.
- For this question, you have been asked to focus on the nature of the market. Try to find some **synonyms** in the text that could be used to describe something as busy or chaotic.
- Think carefully about *how* the writer presents the market as busy. Focus on specific language, phrases and techniques, and evaluate the effects. These may build a particular pace or mood in the text, which can be explored in your answer.
- As you write your response, reuse the words of the question to frame your answer and refer back to the question to remain on task. For example, 'A sense of the market being busy is created by...'.
- Remember Question 4 is asking for your views. Make sure you include some personal comments and evaluations about the text and statement. Use these to help you decide how far you agree with the statement in the question and give reasons to support your answer.

Key terms

evaluate: to form an opinion after thinking about something carefully

synonym: a word that means the same as another word

79

Chapter 3: Component 2

Section A: Question 5

Example Exam Question

| 1 5 | To answer the following questions you must use both texts.

Using information from both texts, explain briefly in your own words what attracts visitors to the markets.

[4 marks]

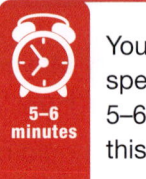

> You should spend about 5–6 minutes on this question.

What is being tested?
- Your ability to select and **synthesise** evidence from different texts. (AO1 2a and b)

Key term

synthesise: to link and put together

What you have to do
- Read the question carefully and work out the specific focus of the question.
- Refer to both texts. Find a couple of examples of evidence from each text to answer the question. You can link similar ideas together.
- Write your response clearly, including the relevant details that you have found in each text.

Tips

- Work out the specific focus of the question: for example, the things that attract visitors to the market. Do not focus on anything else in your response.
- Be mindful of the time as this question is only worth four marks.
- To achieve the most marks, include more than one relevant detail from each text.
- Do not give reasons or detailed explanations; they are not required to answer this question.
- Question 5 is testing how well you select and synthesise evidence from two different texts. Therefore, where possible, try to answer in your own words to show your understanding.
- Quotations are acceptable but never copy large, unselective chunks directly from the text.
- Make sure you do not compare; it is not required to answer Question 5.

Preparing to practise

Section A: Question 6

Example Exam Question

> | 1 | 6 | Both of these texts are about London markets.
>
> Compare:
> - what the two writers experience during their visit
> - how the writers get across their feelings about the markets to their readers
>
> **[10 marks]**
>
> *You must use the text to support your comments and make it clear which text you are referring to.*

10–13 minutes — You should spend about 10–13 minutes on this question.

What is being tested?

- Your ability to compare writers' ideas and **perspectives**, as well as how these are conveyed, across the two texts. (AO3 1a, b, c and d)

What you have to do

- Read the question carefully so you are able to detect if there is a specific focus.
- Use both texts to answer the question.
- Consider the ways in which both writers get across their feelings about each of the markets to the reader.
- Remember to make clear comparisons and contrasts about the two texts and the evidence you select.

Tips

- Question 6 is a comparison question; make sure you constantly focus on comparing the two texts.
- As far as possible, try to give a balanced number of points from each text.
- Make it clear which text or writer you are referring to (and do this throughout your answer). Use the title of each text or the writer's surname explicitly in your response.
- Where possible, include comparative language, for example, 'Text A suggests that… whereas Text B indicates…', 'Although both writers experience…, Mayhew focuses on… unlike Davis who mentions…'.
- Be specific rather than **generalised**: avoid making statements such as 'they both like markets' or 'they both think markets are full of people'.
- Give careful consideration to the second bullet point in the question, and compare how the writers get across their feelings. For example, this could be through the language, the tone used or any personal opinions or observations they make.

Key terms

perspective: a particular attitude towards something or way of regarding something; a point of view

generalised: making a general statement and not looking at the details

Chapter 3: Component 2

Section B: Questions 1 and 2

In this section of the examination, you have two writing tasks to complete.

Example Exam Question

2 1 Write a review for a teenage magazine about the worst book, TV programme or film you have read or watched. Explain why you disliked it and why others should avoid it.

Write your review.

[20 marks]

2 2 'Why would anyone visit a shop or market when we can buy everything online?'

You have been asked to give a talk to people in your class giving your views about the above statement.

Write what you would say in your talk.

[20 marks]

You should aim to spend:
- 5 minutes planning each task
- 25 minutes writing a response to each task

30 minutes

What is being tested?

- Your ability to communicate clearly, effectively and imaginatively, selecting and adapting tone, **style** and **register** for different forms, purposes and audiences. (AO5 1a, b, c)
- Your ability to organise information and ideas, using structural and grammatical features to support coherence and **cohesion** of texts. (AO5 2a, b, c)
- Your ability to use a range of vocabulary and **sentence structures** for clarity, purpose and effect, with accurate spelling and punctuation. (AO6)

What you have to do

- Always spend a few minutes planning a response to the tasks.
- Think about the format for your writing: task 1 is a review and task 2 is a talk.
- Produce a clear and coherent piece of writing for both tasks.
- Write in a suitable tone, style and register for the purpose and audience in the question.
- Structure your writing consciously and effectively and remember to use paragraphs.
- Present your viewpoint persuasively and convincingly.
- Link and develop a range of valid ideas, and use effective and carefully selected vocabulary.
- Use a range of effective technical devices/skills. For example, you might include some **similes**, **imperative verbs** or **rhetorical questions**.
- Write and punctuate your work accurately using a range of sentence structures.

Key terms

style: the way that something is written or presented

register: the level of formality used in writing or the language used by a particular group of people

cohesion: the quality of being logical and consistent

sentence structure: the way in which the words within a sentence (or sentences) are organised

Preparing to practise

Tips

- Focus on each writing task one at a time; you have 30 minutes (including five minutes planning) to spend on each question.
- Your writing in this question is being assessed based on the quality of your content and your ability to write accurately.
- For each of these tasks, you must plan what you are going to write and think carefully about how you will develop the level of detail in each paragraph.
- Look carefully for the audience and purpose of the writing in the question. How will you ensure your writing appeals to them?
- Both tasks require a personal opinion or view. Make sure that you communicate this clearly.
- Leave time at the end to proofread your response, and make corrections or improvements.

Key terms

simile: a figure of speech in which one thing is compared to another using the words 'as' or 'like'

imperative verb: a verb that gives an instruction

rhetorical question: a question that does not need an answer; used to trigger a thought

Activity 1 Answering the sample paper

Using all of the skills and techniques suggested on pages 76–83, complete the exam paper on pages 72–75.

Chapter 3: Component 2

Understanding the mark scheme

A mark scheme is used by examiners and teachers to assess the quality of your response for each question. Understanding the mark scheme can help you to improve the quality of your work as you will know what is needed to gain the highest marks in each question.

Section A: Question 1

Read the sample Question 1 below from the practice exam paper on pages 72–75.

Example Exam Question

1 1 Read the article, 'Camden Market: My Favorite Day Out in London' by Leah Davis.

a) Where did the writer get off the bus? **[1 mark]**

b) What is the name of the Brazilian sweet that the writer cannot resist? **[1 mark]**

c) Which section of the market is Leah Davis' favourite? **[1 mark]**

Key term

indicative content: examples of content that examiners will refer to and you may draw upon as part of a successful answer

This question tests your ability to identify explicit information from a text (AO1, 1a). You will be given this type of question based on both texts in your Component 2 exam. There are three questions, each one usually worth one mark.

Mark scheme

Below is the mark scheme for Question 1 of the sample exam paper. It is a list of **indicative content**.

Award one mark for each correct response in a), b) and c).

a) Camden High Street/near the Camden Town underground (1)
b) Brigadeiros (1)
c) The food court (1)

Improving your Section A: Question 1 response

Activity 2 Self-assessment

1. Look again at your original responses to Question 1. Check the mark scheme above and decide how many marks you would award yourself for your answers.

2. If any of your answers were incorrect, find the correct answer in the source text, circle it and rewrite that response.

Understanding the mark scheme

Upgrade

- Make sure that you use the correct text.
- When you think you have found the correct answer in the text, read the paragraph or sentences around it, to make sure it is definitely correct.

Section A: Question 2

Read the sample Question 2 below from the practice exam paper on pages 72–75.

Example Exam Question

> **1 2** How does the writer try to make Camden Market sound exciting and appealing?
>
> You should comment on:
>
> - what she says
> - her use of language, tone and structure
> - other ways she tries to make the market sound exciting and appealing
>
> [10 marks]

This question tests your ability to explain, comment on and analyse how writers use language and structure to achieve effects and influence readers, using relevant subject terminology where appropriate (AO2 1a, b, c and d). Question 2 is assessed using marking bands: each band contains key words and phrases, which examiners use to decide the mark given to a response. These key words and the criteria for each band can be found in the table below.

Band	Marks	Key words/phrases	Explanation
1	1–2 marks	'simply', 'brief', 'limited'	This means that you are beginning to make one or two straightforward points.
2	3–4 marks	'some', 'simple', 'limited'	This means that your response may include some simple comments and relevant details. Your coverage of the text may be limited.
3	5–6 marks	'commented', 'range', 'begin to show'	This means that you are able to make valid points about a range of examples. You begin to show how features such as words/phrases, tone and structure are used, and you are sometimes able to indicate when a relevant term has been used.
4	7–8 marks	'accurate', 'good range', 'analyse', 'effectively'	This means that you have made sensible and accurate comments about a good range of different examples. You analyse how areas such as language, tone and structure are used to influence the reader. You use subject terminology to support your comments.
5	9–10 marks	'accurate', 'perceptive', 'wide range'	This means that you have made precise and insightful comments about a wide range of different examples. Your response provides detailed analysis. You accurately use relevant subject terminology to support your comments.

Chapter 3: Component 2

Mark scheme

Below is the mark scheme for the sample Question 2 from the practice paper. The key words from each band have been highlighted to help you see how the required level of skill increases, as progress is made through the bands.

Band 1	Give 1–2 marks to those who **simply** identify a few textual details to show that the market was exciting and appealing. These responses are likely to be **brief** and **limited**.
Band 2	Give 3–4 marks to those who identify **some** of the textual details that show the market was exciting and appealing. These responses may include some **simple** comments alongside some relevant selection of detail, although coverage and comments across the whole text may be **limited**. These responses may simply identify some subject terminology.
Band 3	Give 5–6 marks to those who have identified and **commented** on a **range** of examples that Leah Davis uses in the text to show why/how the market was exciting and appealing. These responses **begin to show** how aspects such as language, tone and structure are used to achieve effects and influence the reader. These responses may begin to use relevant subject terminology to support their comments, where appropriate.
Band 4	Give 7–8 marks to those who have made **accurate** comments about a **good range** of different examples that Leah Davis uses in the text to show why/how the market was exciting and appealing. These responses begin to **analyse** how aspects such as language, tone and structure are used to influence the reader. Relevant subject terminology is used to support comments **effectively**, where appropriate.
Band 5	Give 9–10 marks to those who have made **accurate** and **perceptive** comments about a **wide range** of different examples that Leah Davis uses in the text to show why/how the market was exciting and appealing. These responses will provide detailed analysis of how aspects such as language, tone and structure are used to achieve effects and influence readers. Well considered, accurate use of relevant subject terminology supports comments effectively, where appropriate.

The mark scheme also includes a list of indicative content. This provides suggested examples of the content that you may include as part of a successful answer to Question 2. This is not a complete list, but is a good indicator of the most relevant content for the answer. Below, and opposite, is the indicative content list for the sample Question 2.

> **Key terms**
>
> **metaphor:**
> when a thing or person is described as something else for dramatic effect e.g. 'the market was a hive of activity'
>
> **atmosphere:**
> the feeling or mood of a particular place or situation

Details candidates may explore or comment on could be:

- the title shows this is the author's 'Favorite Day Out in London' suggesting it is appealing as it is so highly rated
- the use of direct praise: 'it was amazing'
- the shops are a 'sight to behold' – verb choice here emphasises their visually appealing nature
- positive language describes the buildings: 'brightly… elaborately… serious sensory overload'
- the crowd are appealing to young people or those young at heart: 'a bit on the young side'
- a **metaphor** emphasises many exciting and appealing areas to see: 'just the tip of the iceberg'
- the exaggeration stresses the huge range and adds appeal: 'a million different delicacies'
- the biblical style language used to stress the appealing **atmosphere** of the market: 'behold' 'paradise'
- the use of lists stress the huge range of attractions and furthers the appeal

> - the writer's use of **aside** to make a visit seem increasingly appealing e.g. '(other than food, of course)'
> - the writer confirms that she will definitely visit again
> - the writer ends by telling us she is 'captivated', suggesting she is mesmerised by it all
> - the fluid structure of the text mirrors how she moves from one area to the next
> - the use of lists and rapid pace form part of the structure which creates a busy scene
> - the conclusion of the text mirrors the beginning – both have a positive, jubilant tone
>
> This is not a checklist and the question must be marked in levels of response. Look for and reward valid alternatives.

Sample student responses

Below are extracts from two answers to this question. The first extract is taken from an answer that was given a mark in Band 2 and the second extract is taken from an answer that was given a mark in Band 4.

Student A

The writer tells us that it is her 'favorite day out' so it makes it appealing. She also tells us that it is 'amazing' so we want to visit as it sounds good. Further on in the passage we learn that she thinks that the market is a really pretty place to visit as she tells us it is 'beautiful'. Another thing that is appealing is that the food is cheap as it costs 'around £5 for most dishes'. She makes the market sound appealing as she comments on the 'secret underground tunnel system.' The final exciting thing is that there is 'a new surprise around every corner...'

Student B

Leah Davis makes Camden Market sound appealing beginning with the phrase, 'favorite day out in London' suggesting it is appealing if it is her preferred place. The adjective 'amazing' makes it sound appealing as she holds it in high regard. This positive language continues when she describes the buildings as 'brightly' and the phrase 'just the tip of the iceberg' makes it sound exciting as there are many other fantastic things to see and do. The phrase 'labyrinth of shops' makes the market sound quite exciting – almost like a place where you could easily get lost and with a good deal of mystery and fun. The constant use of listing – from buildings to food types – reinforces the vast array of things to see and do and makes the market sound like a place worth visiting.

> **Key term**
>
> **aside:** a remark that is intended to be heard or noticed by the reader

Activity 3 Building levels of response

1. Look at the two sample answers. Student A was awarded a Band 2 mark for the answer and Student B's answer is part of a Band 4 response. What do you think the key differences are between these two answers? For example, comment on the evidence that has been selected and the level of detail provided.

Chapter 3: Component 2

2. Look again at the mark scheme for this question and focus on Band 5. How could you improve the Band 4 student response to make it a Band 5 answer?

    a. The candidate uses the word 'phrase' on a couple of occasions. What could they use instead?

    b. Does the candidate fully engage with the selected evidence? For example, look at the metaphor 'just the tip of the iceberg'. How can you improve the explanation?

    c. Find some evidence from the text to support the student's final point about the use of lists.

3. Rewrite the Band 4 sample answer, incorporating the advice given above. Include any of your own ideas if they will enhance the answer.

Improving your Section A: Question 2 response

Activity 4 Self-assessment

1. Now look at your original response to Question 2. Compare it to the Band 2 and Band 4 sample answers and then use the mark scheme and indicative content on pages 86–87 to decide which band your response fits into.

2. Think about how you could improve your response.

    a. Is the quality of your analysis consistent throughout?

    b. Have you commented on the tone, language or structure used in the text and how this might make Camden Market appealing?

    c. Do you vary the way in which you refer back to the question (using synonyms instead of repeating 'appealing' and 'exciting')?

    d. Have you linked your ideas so that the whole response sounds fluent?

3. Rewrite your response, paying particular attention to the areas you have identified above that could be developed or improved. Check your revised answer against the mark scheme to see if it would now achieve a higher mark.

Upgrade

- When concluding your response, it is useful to include an overview of the overriding points that have made up your answer. This is a way of reminding the examiner of your main ideas.
- The final bullet point of the exam question asks you to comment on other ways the writer tries to make the market sound exciting and appealing. Include additional techniques or features that the writer has used, for example comment on the use of lists and repetition.

Section A: Question 3

Read the sample Question 3 below from the practice exam paper on pages 72–75.

Example Exam Question

> **1 3** To answer the following questions you will need to read Henry Mayhew's description of the market taken from 'London Labour and the London Poor'.
>
> a) Name one thing that the women were carrying. **[1 mark]**
>
> b) How much does it cost for a 'clean-shaved' chin at the barber's? **[1 mark]**
>
> c) At what time does the market finish? **[1 mark]**

Question 3, like Question 1, tests your ability to **retrieve** information from a text (AO1 1a, b, c and d). The instruction before the question informs you that you are now working on a different text. For Question 3, you are awarded one mark for each correct answer, up to a total of three marks.

Key term

retrieve: to find or extract

Mark scheme

Below is the mark scheme for Question 1 of the sample exam paper. It is a list of indicative content.

> Award one mark for each correct response:
>
> a) White round turnips/cabbages/a piece of red meat (1)
>
> b) A halfpenny (1)
>
> c) 'As the clock strikes eleven' / 11 o'clock / 11 a.m. (1)

Improving your Section A: Question 3 response

Activity 5 Self-assessment

1. Look again at your original responses to Question 3. Decide how many marks you would award yourself. Use the mark scheme to help you make your decision.

2. If any of your answers were incorrect, locate the correct answer in the text and rewrite your response.

Upgrade

- Many candidates find the 19th-century text to be more challenging in terms of language and sentence structures. Look for key words from the question (for example, 'women' and 'barber's') to help you locate the correct details.
- As with Question 1, once you find the correct answer in the text, make sure that you read the text surrounding it to make sure it definitely makes sense as a response to the question.

Chapter 3: Component 2

Section A: Question 4

Read the sample Question 4 below from the practice exam paper on pages 72–75.

> **Example Exam Question**
>
> **1 4** 'Henry Mayhew presents the market as a busy and chaotic place.' How far do you agree with this view?
>
> You should comment on:
> - what he says
> - how it is said
>
> **[10 marks]**
>
> *You must refer to the text to support your comments.*

This question tests your ability to evaluate texts critically and support your comments with appropriate textual references (AO4). Question 4 also requires a personal response alongside some analysis of the text.

Question 4, like Question 2, is assessed using Bands: each band contains key words and phrases, which examiners use to decide the mark given to a response. These key words and the criteria for each band can be found in the table below.

Band	Marks	Key words/phrases	Explanation
1	1–2 marks	'some basic textual details', 'brief', 'limited'	This means that you are beginning to make some simple comments and can back this up with some basic references to the text. Your response may be short and/or lacking in detail.
2	3–4 marks	'a few relevant details', 'a personal response'	This means that your response may include some straightforward comments and pick out a few relevant details from the text. Your coverage of the text may be limited.
3	5–6 marks	'evaluation', 'a range of relevant details', 'personal response'	This means that you are able to identify and comment on a range of examples. You begin to show how areas such as language, tone and structure are used. Your response may begin to use relevant subject terminology.
4	7–8 marks	'critical evaluation', 'a good range of well-selected details', 'understanding'	This means that you have made sensible and accurate comments about a good range of different examples. You analyse how areas such as language, tone and structure are used to influence the reader. You use subject terminology to support your comments.
5	9–10 marks	'detailed and persuasive evaluation', 'convincing, well-selected examples', 'purposeful', 'engagement', 'involvement', 'perceptive'	This means that you have made accurate and perceptive comments about a wide range of different examples, across the whole text. Your response provides detailed analysis. You accurately use relevant subject terminology to support your comments.

Understanding the mark scheme

Mark scheme

Below is the mark scheme for the sample Question 4 from the practice paper. The key words from each band have been highlighted to help you see how the skills level increases, as progress is made through the bands.

Band 1	Give 1–2 marks to those who select some basic textual details and/or express a simple personal opinion. Responses in this band may be brief and limited and /or struggle to engage with the text or the question.
Band 2	Give 3–4 marks to those who select a few relevant details from the text and/or give a personal response to Mayhew's account, although coverage of the whole text may be limited.
Band 3	Give 5–6 marks to those who give an evaluation of the text supported by a range of relevant details from across the text. These responses will show some critical awareness and exploration of Mayhew's account that inform a personal response.
Band 4	Give 7–8 marks to those who give a detailed, critical evaluation of the text and its effects, supported by a good range of well-selected details from across the text. Personal response comments will be linked to a critical awareness and understanding of Mayhew's account.
Band 5	Give 9–10 marks to those who give a detailed and persuasive evaluation of the text and its effects, supported by convincing, well-selected examples and purposeful textual references. These responses will show engagement and involvement, where candidates take an overview to make perceptive comments and evaluation of Mayhew's account.

The mark scheme also contains a list of indicative content. This provides suggested examples of the content that you may draw upon as part of a successful answer. There will be valid alternatives that you may have used, but it is a really good indicator of the most relevant content for the answer. Below is the indicative content list for Question 4.

Details that candidates may evaluate or give a personal response to could be:

- Mayhew's building of the noise from 'scarcely heard' to 'low hum' to 'noisy shouting' is detailed to create a clear sense of him being enveloped by sound

- the use of language linked to sound to create a busy, chaotic atmosphere: 'hubbub', 'din', 'confusion', 'a thousand voices bellowing'.

- the movement of the women who 'run to and fro,' with various food items sounds busy and frantic

- the verb used to describe the women as 'streaming forth with bags of flour in their hands,' creates an image of intensity and speed which adds to the chaotic nature

- the noise continues without respite: 'Walnuts, blacking, apples, onions, braces, combs, turnips, herrings, pens and corn-plaster, are all bellowed out at the same time'

- the description of the rubbish creates an untidy and chaotic image for the reader: 'The pavement is green with the refuse leaves of vegetables'

- even children are present and moving quickly: 'Boys are running home…'

- the market sounds loud and frantic: 'the bustle doubles itself, the cries grow louder, the confusion greater', emphasising the constant and growing chaos

- women 'push their way through the throng', suggesting an increasing sense of urgency

- the text begins and ends in calm – a clear contrast to the chaos in the mid-section of the text, which only serves to present the market as more intense and busier

This is not a checklist and the question must be marked in levels of response. Look for and reward valid alternatives.

Chapter 3: Component 2

Sample student responses

Below are extracts from two different answers to this question. The first response has been awarded a Band 3 mark and the second response has been awarded a Band 5 mark.

Student A

A chaotic scene is presented through the description of the people, 'streaming forth with bags of flour in their hands' because the verb 'streaming' makes it sound like people are literally flooding the streets and causing congestion. An additional description says the women 'push their way through the throng', which makes it sounds like a battle as they need to 'push' against others to navigate the densely packed streets. The noun 'throng' adds to the sense of crowding and intensifies the chaotic and busy description.

Student B

The whole place sounds very busy. The women are described as 'streaming forth with bags of flour in their hands,' and this makes it sound like the whole place is crammed with people and produce. The women are later described as pushing 'their way through the throng' and this gives the sense that the whole place is extremely busy as people are having to push and shove to get past other people. The word 'throng' also makes it sound very busy as this is used to describe really busy places.

Activity 6 Building levels of response

1. Look at the two sample answers. Student A was awarded a Band 3 mark for their answer and Student B's answer is part of a Band 5 response. What are the key differences between them? Complete the following steps:

   a. Underline where the students have included evidence from the text.

   b. Highlight where the student has commented on the writer's ideas.

   c. Circle where the students have commented on the writer's methods.

2. Choose one of the bullet points from the indicative content list. Write two sentences to explain how this creates a busy, chaotic atmosphere. Refer to the mark scheme on page 91 to ensure your response will achieve a high mark.

Understanding the mark scheme

Improving your Section A: Question 4 response

Activity 7 Self-assessment

1. Look again at your original response to Question 4. Refer to the Band 3 and Band 5 sample answers, as well as the mark scheme and indicative content on page 91, and decide which mark your answer would be given.

2. Think about which areas of your response you could develop in order to improve it. Consider the following:

   a. Have you made it clear how far you agree that Mayhew presents the market as a busy, chaotic place?

   b. Have you considered how the pace and tone varies throughout the text, and commented on why the writer might have taken that approach to convey a busy, chaotic atmosphere?

   c. Have you carefully considered the language that the writer uses to build atmosphere?

3. Rewrite your response, paying particular attention to the areas you have identified above that could be developed or improved, and considering the Upgrade panel. Check your revised answer against the mark scheme to see if it would now achieve a higher mark.

Upgrade

- Remember to link your ideas together when talking about the whole text for this question. Look at the table below for language that you could use to link similar and different points, as you demonstrate how far you agree with the view stated in the question.

Words to link similar points	Words to link different points
similarly, comparatively, in addition, likewise, equally, as well as, both, equivalent, furthermore, also, as well as, moreover	alternatively, in contrast, however, nevertheless, on the contrary, on the other hand, although, however, oppose, unlike, whereas, besides

- Constantly probe why certain words and phrases have been used; these are deliberate decisions made by the writer to achieve effects. For example, this writer uses the verb 'sally' (line 9) to suggest that the men are rushing with purpose, and therefore portrayed as important.

Chapter 3: Component 2

Section A: Question 5

Read the sample Question 5 below from the practice exam paper on pages 72–75.

Example Exam Question

> **1 5** To answer the following questions you must use both texts.
>
> Using information from both texts, explain briefly in your own words what attracts visitors to the markets. **[4 marks]**

This question tests your ability to select and synthesise evidence from both texts (AO1 2a and b). You need to use a few details or ideas from each text to answer the question. Because this question is worth four marks, there are only four marking bands so a table to analyse the mark scheme has not been included.

Mark scheme

Below is the mark scheme for the sample Question 5 from the practice paper. Some key words from each band have been highlighted to help you see how the skills level increases, as progress is made through the bands.

Band 1	Give 1 mark to those who struggle to offer a relevant detail from each of the texts or offer relevant detail from just **one** text.
Band 2	Give 2 marks to those who select at least a relevant detail from each of the texts.
Band 3	Give 3 marks to those who select relevant details from both texts.
Band 4	Give 4 marks to those who synthesise with clear understanding and provide an overview drawn from a range of relevant details from both texts.

The mark scheme also includes a list of indicative content. This provides suggested examples of the content that you may include as part of a successful answer to Question 5. This is not a complete list, but is a good indicator of the most relevant content for the answer. Below is the indicative content list for Question 5.

> Details that candidates may select, explore or respond to could be:
>
> | Both focus on the different buildings and areas that food can be purchased/the variety on offer ||
> |---|---|
> | **Davis:** <ul><li>brightly painted storefronts and 'elaborate sculptures'</li><li>an array of shops, pubs, etc</li><li>beautiful market halls</li><li>huge variety of eating places 'covered' and with so many options</li><li>historic area with 'stables'</li></ul> | **Mayhew:** <ul><li>women have their 'filled aprons' as plenty of food types on offer</li><li>butchers and coal shed are 'filled' with customers</li><li>the 'shut-up baker's' has people 'streaming' through the doors</li><li>the halfpenny barber's is 'busy'</li><li>wide range of food types listed to emphasise the range on offer</li></ul> |
>
> This is not a checklist and the question must be marked in levels of response. Look for and reward valid alternatives.

Understanding the mark scheme

Sample student answers

Below are extracts from two different answers to this question. The first extract is taken from an answer that was given a mark in Band 4 and the second extract is taken from an answer that was given a mark in Band 1.

Student A

The two markets are both full of different things that would attract a visitor and it is clear in both texts that many choose to visit the wide range of attractions on offer. Despite being written over 100 years apart, the attractions very much centre on food items and shopping. Davis describes a vibrant and lively place filled with diverse structures ranging from 'kitschy tourist shops' to 'fruit juice stands'. The vast array of eateries with 'just about every corner of the globe represented' are an attractive proposition for visitors. The shops are described as 'wacky' and 'varied' emphasising the wide range of attractions on offer. Like Davis, Mayhew focuses on the physical aspects of the market that attract visitors. The wide range of food choices, such as 'walnuts', and 'apples, onions', as well as the sheer volume of people who seek to visit 'the barber's,' 'the coal shed' etc, suggests that the market is incredibly popular.

Student B

They both have lots of things on offer for people so they want to come and visit. Davis says 'options' and Mayhew tells us that there are lots of different types of food that people want to come and buy.

> ### ✏️ Activity 8 Building levels of response
>
> 1. Student A's response was marked in Band 4 (remember that this is the top band for this question). Using the Band 4 criteria, annotate the response and see if you can work out where and why they were awarded four marks.
>
>   a. Underline where it shows clear understanding of the text.
>
>   b. Circle an overview point that has been included.
>
>   c. Highlight the range in relevant details that has been included from both texts.
>
> 2. Student B's response was marked in Band 1. What advice would you give to this candidate to help them improve their answer? Use the questions below to guide your thinking:
>
>   a. Are they focusing on the question?
>
>   b. Have they selected relevant evidence from each text that links to the question?
>
>   c. Do they show clear understanding?

Chapter 3: Component 2

Improving your Section A: Question 5 response

Activity 9 Self-assessment

1. Look again at your original response to Question 5. Compare it to the Band 1 and Band 4 sample answers, and refer to the mark scheme and indicative content on page 94. Decide which mark your response would be given.

2. Think about which parts of your response you could develop in order to improve it. Look in particular at the quality of what you have written about the individual texts.

    a. Have you included a similar level of evidence and detail about each text?

    b. Do you cover a range of details from each text? If not, look again at the indicative content and choose one additional area that you could add for each text.

    c. The focus of the question was 'what attracts visitors'. Have you given sufficient consideration to this part of the question? Have you used the word 'attracts' or similar synonyms in your answer?

    d. Reread the two articles. Highlight any additional aspects of the two markets that might attract people to visit them.

    e. Consider the advice in the upgrade panel.

3. Rewrite your response, paying particular attention to the areas you have identified above that could be developed or improved. Check your revised answer against the mark scheme to see if it would now achieve a higher mark.

Upgrade

- Remind yourself of the definition of synthesise: to bring together information from different sources to create a new text. Make sure you comment on both texts and try to cover them in the same level of detail.
- Make it clear which text you got the information from by referring to the writer's surname or title of the text.
- Refer back to the phrasing of the question throughout your answer to keep your answer focused.

Section A: Question 6

Read the sample Question 6 below from the practice exam paper on pages 72–75.

Example Exam Question

> **1 6** Both of these texts are about London markets.
>
> Compare:
>
> - what the two writers experience during their visit
> - how the writers get across their feelings about the markets to their readers
>
> **[10 marks]**
>
> *You must use the text to support your comments and make it clear which text you are referring to.*

This question tests your ability to compare writers' ideas and perspectives, as well as how these are conveyed, across the two texts in your exam paper (AO3). Question 6 is assessed using marking bands: each band contains key words and phrases, which examiners use to decide the mark given to a response. These key words and the criteria for each band can be found in the table below.

Band	Marks	Key words/phrases	Explanation
1	1–2 marks	'basic similarity or difference', 'not clear'	This means that you may not make it clear which text is being referred to. You will have limited focus and may make limited comparisons.
2	3–4 marks	'some similarities and differences', 'some evidence', 'some focus'	This means that you use some evidence to make some comparisons. You might attempt to comment on how the writers get across their ideas.
3	5–6 marks	'identify similarities and differences', 'appropriate comments'	This means that you find features to compare and contrast both texts and make some relevant comments on how the writers get across their experiences.
4	7–8 marks	'detailed comparisons', 'range of valid comments'	This means that you explain comparisons and analyse how the writers get across their experiences.
5	9–10 marks	'comparisons that are sustained and detailed', 'clear understanding', 'wide range'	This means that you make detailed comparisons throughout your answer and go on to show a clear understanding of the different ways in which the writers get across their experiences through lots of different valid comments.

Understanding the mark scheme

97

Chapter 3: Component 2

Mark scheme

Below is the mark scheme for the sample Question 6 from the practice paper. The key words from each band have been highlighted to help you see how the skills required increase, as progress is made through the bands.

Band 1	Give 1–2 marks to those who identify a basic similarity and/or difference in what the texts say about what could be experienced at the markets. Marks in this band may only deal with one text or not make it clear which text is being referred to.
Band 2	Give 3–4 marks to those who identify and give a straightforward description of some similarities and differences in what the texts say about what could be experienced at the markets. Some evidence will be used to support ideas and comparisons. Some focus on how the writers get across their ideas may be emerging.
Band 3	Give 5–6 marks to those who identify similarities and differences in what the texts say about what could be experienced at the markets and make some appropriate comments on how the writers get across their experiences to their readers.
Band 4	Give 7–8 marks to those who make detailed comparisons about what could be experienced at the markets and offer a range of valid comments about how the writers get across their experiences to their readers.
Band 5	Give 9–10 marks to those who make comparisons that are sustained and detailed about what could be seen and experienced at the markets and go on to show a clear understanding of the different ways in which the writers get across their experiences to their readers through a wide range of valid comments.

The mark scheme also includes a list of indicative content. This provides suggested examples of the content that you may include as part of a successful answer to Question 6. This is not a complete list, but is a good indicator of the most relevant content for the answer. Below is the indicative content list for the sample Question 6.

> **Key term**
>
> **first person:** when we use 'I' or 'we' as the narrative voice in a text

Details that candidates may explore or comment on could be:

1. What the writers experienced

Davis:
- a sense of familiarity: 'I felt right at home'
- excessive quantities: 'serious sensory overload', 'a million different delicacies'
- juxtaposition in 'friendly strangers' reinforce the unexpectedly positive visit
- 'I couldn't help…' conveys an element of ease in the visit
- 'a lot of walking to do' shows commitment to see everything
- she is marvelling at everything there is to look at in positive language and personification: 'captivated', 'plenty of shiny things vying for your attention'

Mayhew:
- a constant development of noise, from 'scarcely heard' to 'bellowing'
- busy and intense/frantic atmosphere, constant movement: 'crowded', 'run', 'streaming'
- wide range of different people: 'boys', 'labourers and mechanics', women running, the 'apple-man'
- the intense trading and touting for business: 'shouts'
- the continuation of noise from the church bells to the 'bustle of people'
- peace: 'the Sunday's rest begins'

Understanding the mark scheme

2. How they get across their feelings to their readers	
Davis:	**Mayhew:**
• she embarks on her trip with no planning or expectations, so her experience feels unexpectedly positive • she constantly conveys a genuine sense of awe and wonder about every aspect of the market; observational style • she marvels at what can be seen from the elaborate sculptures to the 'stable' area • the constant use of **first person** to convey feelings and reactions to what is experienced • the wealth of positive language to convey the experience as an extremely positive one • repetition of verb 'wandered' almost feels like we are stumbling across these wonders alongside the writer • use of aside/**parenthesis** to give personal views effectively conveys her feelings	• use of **present tense** to capture the frenetic, chaotic nature of the market • the writer does not give any direct indication of his feelings, but concentrates on observing what can be seen in a very **unbiased** fashion • the constant use of verbs to describe rapid movement perfectly conveys their experience as a lively and dynamic one • the writer begins and ends with peace, which is an excellent contrast to the chaotic market • the writer focuses on many people to create a realistic sense of the crowded area

This is not a checklist and the question must be marked in levels of response. Look for and reward valid alternatives.

Sample student answers

Below are extracts from two different answers to this question. The first extract is taken from an answer that was given a mark in Band 3 and the second extract is taken from an answer that was given a mark in Band 5.

Student A

In this extract, the two writers, Davis and Mayhew, both focus quite a lot on the food that can be bought at the different markets. Davis focuses on the food that she buys in a food court, where she just loves the food that is on offer, for example, 'I just couldn't resist'. She then tells us about lots of different food types from around the world. In Mayhew's text, there is also a focus on food but it is more about the food that people are buying to eat at home, not the food that can be eaten on the streets, for example 'cabbages under their arms' and 'herring held in a piece of paper'. Both writers get across the interest in food by telling us in lots of detail about what can be bought.

Key terms

parenthesis: an additional word, phrase or sentence inserted into a passage that is grammatically complete without it, marked off by brackets, dashes or commas

present tense: a tense which expresses a current activity or action

unbiased: fair and does not support or favour a particular group

Chapter 3: Component 2

Student B

Both writers comment on the food in the markets. For Davis, this is experienced in a food court where she marvels at the vast range of food ('Korean, French, Venezuelan...'), the cheap prices ('around £5 for most dishes') and the appealing nature of the food, for example 'I just couldn't resist'. Davis conveys her feelings about the food with a great deal of enthusiasm by including lists of the wide range on offer, and making positive observations, for example 'something for everyone'. In Mayhew's text, there is no mention of food as something to be consumed sociably at the market, it is merely something to be purchased for consumption later. While Davis' experience is personally enjoyable, Mayhew's experience is far more observational as he comments on the frantic grabbing of food, for example, 'cabbages under their arms' and 'herring held in a piece of paper'. Like Davis, he also focuses on the types of places available for purchasing food, such as 'the baker's' and the 'cabbage-barrow'.

Activity 10 Building levels of response

1. Look at the two sample answers: Student A was awarded a Band 3 mark for the answer and Student B's answer is part of a Band 5 response. What are the key differences between these answers? Complete the following:

   a. Underline where an effective comparison has been made between the texts in both responses.

   b. Circle where textual references have been included in both responses.

   c. Highlight where the student has commented on the effects of the writer's language in both responses.

   d. Tick the words or phrases that make it clear which text the student is referring to.

2. Select a piece of indicative content from the list on pages 98–99. Follow the steps below to help you build a response to compare this in the two texts.

   a. Write down a sentence to compare or contrast this idea between the two source texts.

   b. Find some evidence in the both texts to support the point you have selected.

   c. Analyse this evidence and comment on how the information is conveyed.

   d. Try to add some subject terminology, if relevant, into your sentence.

Improving your Section A: Question 6 response

Activity 11 Self-assessment

1. Look again at your original response to Question 6. Compare it to the Band 3 and Band 5 sample answers, and the mark scheme and indicative content on pages 98–99. Decide which mark your response would be given.

2. Think about which parts of your response you could improve. Look in particular at the quality of what you have written about the individual texts.

   a. Have you remained focused on the comparison element of the question?
   b. Have you given a balanced answer, focusing on each of the texts equally?
   c. Have you produced a balanced answer by giving a similar level of attention to each of the texts?
   d. Have you included a range of points, rather than focusing on just one idea?
   e. Have you explored each point in detail and included evidence to support your findings?

3. Rewrite your response, paying particular attention to the areas you have identified above. Check your revised answer against the mark scheme to see if it would now achieve a higher mark.

Upgrade

- Remember to think about the writer's methods. Consider how they put the information together and the techniques and language choices they used.
- Remember this is a comparative task. Use language to compare and contrast in your answer; there are some examples of this on page 93.
- Make sure you have left enough time to complete Question 6.

Chapter 3: Component 2

Section B: Questions 1 and 2

Read the sample Question 1 and Question 2 below from Section B of the practice exam paper on pages 72–75.

> **Example Exam Question**
>
> **2 1** Write a review for a teenage magazine about the worst book, TV programme or film you have read or watched. Explain why you disliked it and why others should avoid it.
>
> Write your review.
>
> **[20 marks]**
>
> **2 2** 'Why would anyone visit a shop or market when we can buy everything online?'
>
> You have been asked to give a talk to people in your class giving your views about the above statement.
>
> Write what you would say in your talk.
>
> **[20 marks]**

These questions test your ability to:

- communicate clearly, effectively and imaginatively, selecting and adapting tone, style and register for different forms, purposes and audiences (AO5)
- organise information and ideas, using structural and grammatical features to support coherence and cohesion of texts (AO5)
- use a range of vocabulary and sentence structures for clarity, purpose and effect, with accurate spelling and punctuation (AO6).

Question 1 and 2 in Section B of the Component 2 exam paper are worth 20 marks each. The mark scheme is divided into two sections to reflect the two assessment objectives. Of the 20 marks available for each writing question, the quality of your communication and organisation (AO5) is worth 12 marks for each task, and the quality of your vocabulary, sentence structure, spelling and punctuation (AO6) is worth eight marks for each task.

> **Tip**
>
> Unlike in Component 1, *both* writing tasks must be completed in Component 2. You have approximately one hour to complete both writing tasks, so you should aim to spend 5 minutes planning and 25 minutes writing each response.

Understanding the mark scheme

Communication and Organisation (AO5)

The mark scheme for Communication and Organisation (AO5) is divided into marking bands: each band contains key words and phrases, which examiners use to decide the mark given to a response. These key words and the criteria for each band can be found in the table below.

Band	Key Words	Explanation
1	'basic awareness', 'content may be thin and brief'	This means that your writing is quite simple and is not always organised in a way that makes sense. You may make some points clearly. Your reader struggles to follow what you have written and meaning is hindered by the inaccuracy of the writing. Your writing may be brief and undeveloped.
2	'awareness', 'limited development', 'some sequencing', 'fluency'	This means that your writing is sometimes clear and sometimes makes sense. Your writing is sometimes organised and some ideas are developed sensibly. You have tried to be clear in the way you put across your ideas but may not always be successful. Sometimes the reader may struggle to understand or lose the sense of your points/ideas.
3	'clear understanding', 'appropriately adapted', 'communication has clarity and fluency'	This means that your writing is mostly clear with appropriate reasons. You organise your writing with a sense of purpose and your writing is coherent. These answers will include a range of sensible details and will be clear. The writing will be mostly fluent and will interest a reader. There will be a clear awareness of the intended reader throughout.
4	'consistent understanding', 'secure awareness', 'well-judged and detailed', 'coherently developed'	This means that your writing is consistent, clear and well-judged. You organise your writing with clarity and you use language carefully to communicate your ideas. Your ideas are coherently developed, effective and relevant to the task. You have a secure awareness of your reader.
5	'sophisticated', 'sustained', 'confidently', 'ambitious, pertinent', 'convincingly developed'	This means that your writing has been crafted with confidence and ambition. You structure writing effectively and are willing to be ambitious and sophisticated in your use of language and ideas. You are able to fully engage your reader and develop your ideas with convincing details.

Below, and on page 104, is the mark scheme for Communication and Organisation (AO5) for Section B: Questions 1 and 2 of the practice paper on pages 72–75. The key words from each band have been highlighted to help you see how the skills level increases, as progress is made through the bands.

Band 1	**1–2 marks** • basic awareness of the purpose and format of the task • some basic awareness of the reader/intended audience • some attempt to adapt register to purpose/audience • some relevant content despite uneven coverage of the topic • content may be thin and brief • simple sequencing of ideas (paragraphs may be used to show obvious divisions or group ideas into some order) • there is some basic clarity but communication of meaning is limited
Band 2	**3–4 marks** • shows some understanding of the purpose and format of the task • shows awareness of the reader/intended audience • a clear attempt to adapt register to purpose/audience • some reasons are given in support of opinions/ideas • limited development of ideas • some sequencing of ideas into paragraphs (structure/direction may be uncertain) • communication has some clarity and fluency

103

Chapter 3: Component 2

Band 3	**5–7 marks** • shows ==clear understanding== of the purpose and format of the task • shows clear awareness of the reader/intended audience • register is ==appropriately adapted== to purpose/audience • content is developed and appropriate reasons are given in support of opinions/ideas • ideas are organised into coherent arguments • there is some shape and structure in the writing (paragraphs are used to give sequence and organisation) • ==communication has clarity and fluency==
Band 4	**8–10 marks** • shows ==consistent understanding== of the purpose and format of the task • shows ==secure awareness== of the reader/intended audience • register is appropriately and consistently adapted to purpose/audience • content is ==well-judged and detailed== • ideas are organised and ==coherently developed== with supporting detail • there is clear shape and structure in the writing (paragraphs are used effectively to give sequence and organisation) • communication has clarity, fluency and some ambition
Band 5	**11–12 marks** • shows ==sophisticated== understanding of the purpose and format of the task • shows ==sustained== awareness of the reader/intended audience • appropriate register is ==confidently== adapted to purpose/audience • content is ==ambitious==, ==pertinent== and sophisticated • ideas are ==convincingly developed== and supported by a range of relevant details • there is sophistication in the shape and structure of the writing • communication has ambition and sophistication

Vocabulary, Sentence structure, Spelling and Punctuation (AO6)

The mark scheme for Vocabulary, Sentence structure, Spelling and Punctuation (AO6) is also divided into five marking bands: each band contains key words and phrases, which examiners use to decide the mark given to a response. These key words and the criteria for each band can be found in the table below.

Band	Key words/phrases	Explanation
1	'limited range', 'control', 'some attempt'	This means that your writing is not very accurate. Your spelling and use of punctuation and grammar contain basic errors that hinder the meaning and/or your sentences lack variety. If you were to underline all of the errors in your work there would probably be a lot of areas underlined in your writing.
2	'some variety', 'control', 'usually accurate', 'generally secure', 'some range'	This means that your writing is sometimes accurate. Spelling, punctuation and grammar are sometimes controlled but there will be increasing errors across multiple areas (e.g. spelling, grammar and punctuation). Your use of vocabulary shows some range but this may be simple and/or have mixed success.
3	'variety in sentence structure', 'mostly secure', 'accurately', 'beginning to develop'	This means that your writing is mostly accurate and reliable. Spelling, punctuation and grammar are mostly controlled. Your use of vocabulary is beginning to show care and some thought.
4	'varied', 'secure', 'range used'	This means that your writing is generally very accurate and reliable. Spelling, punctuation and grammar are accurate and care has been taken. Your use of vocabulary is careful and thoughtful.
5	'appropriate and effective variation', 'controlled and accurate', 'confidently', 'totally secure', 'wide range', 'ambitious'	This means that your writing is extremely accurate. Errors rarely occur and your writing is technically sophisticated and carefully crafted for effect. You can use a wide range of carefully chosen vocabulary for maximum effect.

Understanding the mark scheme

Below is the mark scheme for Vocabulary, Sentence structure, Spelling and Punctuation (AO6) for Section B: Questions 1 and 2 of the practice paper on pages 72–75. The key words from each band have been highlighted to help you see how the skills level increases, as progress is made through the bands.

Band 1	**1 mark** • limited range of sentence structure • control of sentence construction is limited • there is some attempt to use punctuation • some spelling is accurate • control of tense and agreement is limited • limited range of vocabulary
Band 2	**2–3 marks** • some variety of sentence structure • there is some control of sentence construction • some control of a range of punctuation • the spelling is usually accurate • control of tense and agreement is generally secure • there is some range of vocabulary
Band 3	**4–5 marks** • there is variety in sentence structure • control of sentence construction is mostly secure • a range of punctuation is used, mostly accurately • most spelling, including that of irregular words, is correct • control of tense and agreement is mostly secure • vocabulary is beginning to develop and is used with some precision
Band 4	**6–7 marks** • sentence structure is varied to achieve particular effects • control of sentence construction is secure • a range of punctuation is used accurately • spelling, including that of irregular words, is secure • control of tense and agreement is secure • vocabulary is ambitious and used with precision
Band 5	**8 marks** • there is appropriate and effective variation of sentence structures • virtually all sentence construction is controlled and accurate • a range of punctuation is used confidently and accurately • virtually all spelling, including that of complex irregular words, is correct • control of tense and agreement is totally secure • a wide range of appropriate, ambitious vocabulary is used to create effect or convey precise meaning

Chapter 3: Component 2

Improving your Section B: Questions 1 and 2 responses

✏ Activity 12 Self-assessment

1. Now read your original responses to Section B: Questions 1 and 2. Refer back to the mark scheme for Communication and Organisation (AO5) on pages 103–104. Decide which mark your response would be given.

2. Think about how you could improve the content and organisation of your response. Consider the bullet points below:

    Organisation:
    - Did you write a plan for each task to help you organise and sequence your ideas?
    - Have you structured your writing in a way that is suitable for its purpose?
    - Have you included an engaging opening and closing?
    - Have you linked your ideas and included paragraphs to build a convincing argument?

    Communication:
    - Have you included some suitable features for a review or a talk, for example, a bold opening statement or engaging title, range of personal reflections, personal pronouns and facts, to engage your reader/audience?
    - Have you ensured the content, tone and language is suitable for the audience of the magazine or the people receiving the talk? (Remember that this is still being assessed by an examiner.)
    - Have you supported your viewpoint with rhetorical questions?
    - Have you written in sufficient detail and developed a range of interesting ideas?
    - Have you included rhetorical questions, facts or **anecdotes** to support your viewpoint?

3. Now refer to the mark scheme for Vocabulary, Sentence structure, Spelling and Punctuation (AO6) on page 105. Review each sentence of your writing, and decide which mark your response would be given based on this mark scheme.

Understanding the mark scheme

4. Think about how your technical accuracy could be improved. Check the following:

   a. Have you spelled all topic-specific vocabulary correctly?
   b. Have you used a range of different punctuation types, for example, full stops, questions marks and commas?
   c. Have you varied the length and order of your sentences?
   d. Are your sentences grammatically accurate so the meaning is clear?
   e. Have you used **tenses** and verb agreement correctly in your writing?

5. Rewrite your responses, paying particular attention to the areas you have identified that could be developed, corrected and improved. Check your revised answers against the mark schemes to see if they would now achieve higher marks.

Key terms

anecdote: an amusing or interesting story about a real incident or person

tenses: the form of verbs used to show the time of the action, in the past, present or future

Upgrade

- Before you begin, know the purpose and exact audience of your writing. What are you trying to achieve? How are you going to achieve it?
- Establish a suitable tone in your writing: if you are writing a negative review, include some suitably negative language, for example, 'dreadful', 'awful' and 'appalling'.
- Remember to spend approximately five minutes planning your work and one or two minutes checking your writing at the end.
- Be mindful of the common errors that you make. Review your work and see if your teacher has indicated any errors, for example, confusion with tenses, comma splicing, inaccurate apostrophes or incorrect use of semi-colons.

Chapter 4: Component 2

Component 2 sample exam paper

The following account has been taken from an article by Max Campbell and is about his experience of sailing alone across the Atlantic.

Sailing Solo Across the Atlantic

Max Campbell, 21, began sailing in Bristol Harbour at the age of five. In 2015 he bought *Flying Cloud* and sailed her single-handed to the Caribbean.

As I passed the halfway point, I noticed a few grey clouds in the eastern sky. There had been no rain since the Canaries and as the isolated cluster grew nearer, I could see they were blanketed by a misty haze – quite a contrast to the white, fluffy cumulus clouds I had become so used to seeing. The **squall** brought an increase in wind and a heavy downpour. In the unfamiliar conditions, I struggled on the foredeck to remove the pole and lash down one of the **genoas**, but before I had finished, it had passed and I found myself becalmed.

In the following days, the **squalls** became more and more frequent. In daylight I could spot them on the horizon, dark shapes creeping up from behind like a pack of wolves. I could sense their presence at night too, either by the light rain blowing through the companionway, or the slight increase in wind. Prewarned, I would jump out of the cabin and take in sail, but one **squall** succeeded in catching me off guard [...]. Both sails and poles came crashing down to the deck. Lesson well and truly learned. [...]

After 18 days at sea, I could feel the presence of land looming in the distance. I noticed more seabirds circling around the boat and even saw some commercial shipping. With 200 miles to go I felt on top of the world. In my mind, there was no possibility of not making it, whatever came my way. But I had tempted fate, and now it would punish me with fury.

While priming the paraffin stove, a flaming bottle of methylated spirit exploded in my hand with a squeaky pop. Barely clothed and covered in flames, searing pain ravaged my face and torso. I rushed outside and held onto a stanchion, grasping for my life as I flipped myself over the side. Extinguished, I climbed back on board and assessed the damage. My duvet and other items of clothing had caught fire, so I threw a bucket of water down the companionway to douse the flames, but it was obvious that the worst of the damage had been inflicted on my body. Charred pieces of skin fell off my arms, chest, and torso, my face felt stiff, and several big blisters had already formed.

My days of working for the RNLI [charity] had prepared me well for this situation, but I never foresaw having to treat myself. I used dressings, creams, antibiotics and painkillers, making myself look more like a bandaged mummy] than a sailor. [...]

My arrival in the Caribbean was not as I had hoped it would be. It was a relief to be back on land, but I felt completely robbed of celebration. I dropped anchor within a stone's throw of the shore, then struggled to pack the boat away and pump up the dinghy. Two hours later I lay dressed like a mummy in a hospital bed. [...]

The burns were superficial, so I remind myself that it was a small setback, and that although it was the end of the journey, it is not the end of the adventure. The more time that passes, the better I am able to [...] focus more on the 5,000 miles covered during the first seven amazing months. I still love adventure and the ocean. Single-handed sailing offers incredible, euphoric joy, and I'm eager for the next voyage.

- -

squall: a storm or a sudden gust of wind
genoas: a large sail, used especially on yachts

In 1898, Joshua Slocum embarked on a journey around the world in a 37-foot yacht called the Spray. Slocum kept a diary documenting his travels. In this extract he sails into Port Angosto during a snowstorm.

Sailing Alone Around the World

I was sailing in the open Pacific Ocean when another gale had sprung up, but the wind was still fair, and I had only twenty-six miles to run for Port Angosto, a dreary enough place, where, however, I would find a safe harbour in which to refit and stow cargo. I carried on sailing to make the harbour before dark, and she fairly flew along, all covered with snow, which fell thick and fast, till she looked like a white winter bird. Between the storm-bursts I saw the headland of my port, and was steering for it when a sudden blast of wind caught the mainsail, flipped it over, and dear! dear! how nearly was this the cause of disaster; for the sheet parted and a pole unshipped, and it was then close upon night. I worked till the perspiration poured from my body to get things adjusted and in working order before dark, and above all, to get it done before the boat drove downwind of the port of refuge. Even then I did not get the pole shipped back in its saddle. I was at the entrance of the harbour before I could get this done, and it was time to haul her to or miss the port; but in that condition, like a bird with a broken wing, she made the haven. The accident which so **jeopardised** my vessel and cargo was caused by a **defective** sheet-rope, one made from **sisal**, a treacherous fiber which has caused a deal of strong language among sailors.

I did not run the Spray into the inner harbour of Port Angosto, but came to inside a bed of seaweed under a steep cliff on the port side going in. It was an exceedingly snug nook, and to make doubly sure of holding on here against the gale force wind I moored her with two anchors and secured her, besides, by cables to trees.

---

jeopardised: to threaten or put at risk

defective: something that is faulty or imperfect

sisal: fibre from the sisal plant which is used when making ropes or matting

SECTION A: 40 Marks

*Answer **all** the following questions.*

Read the article, 'Sailing Solo Across the Atlantic' by Max Campbell.

1.1 a) How many miles did Max Campbell have left of his journey when the accident occurred? [1]

b) Name one thing that caught fire when the bottle of methylated spirit exploded. [1]

c) Which famous charity did Max Campbell previously work for? [1]

1.2 How does Max Campbell try to show that his journey was dramatic?

You should comment on:

- what he says
- his use of language, tone and structure
- other ways that make his account sound dramatic [10]

To answer the following questions you will need to read Captain Joshua Slocum's account of 'Sailing Alone Around the World'.

1.3 a) In which ocean is Captain Joshua Slocum sailing? [1]

b) How far away was Port Angosto? [1]

c) How did Captain Joshua Slocum secure his boat when he reached Port Angosto? [1]

1.4 'In this extract, Captain Joshua Slocum faces some difficult conditions.' How far do you agree with this view?

You should comment on:

- what he says
- how it is said [10]

You must refer to the text to support your comments.

To answer the following questions you must use both texts.

1.5 Using information from both texts, explain briefly in your own words how the two sailors reacted to the weather conditions. [4]

1.6 Both of these texts describe a solo yacht journey.

Compare:

- what Captain Joshua Slocum and Max Campbell did during their journeys
- how the writers try to convey the dangers of what they did [10]

You must use the text to support your comments and make it clear which text you are referring to.

SECTION B: 40 marks

Answer Question 1 and Question 2.

For each question, 12 marks are awarded for communication and organisation; 8 marks are awarded for vocabulary, sentence structure, punctuation and spelling.

Think about the purpose and audience for your writing.

You should aim to write about 300–400 words for each task.

2.1 This is part of an article that appeared in a newspaper:
'All young people should be encouraged to take a gap year or do something adventurous.'

Write a letter to the newspaper giving your views on this subject. [20]

2.2 Write a lively article for your school or college magazine with the heading:
'A healthy mind is just as important as a healthy body.'

Write your article. [20]

Chapter 4: Component 2

Preparing to practise

Before you try to complete this practice exam paper, you should think carefully about what skills are being tested in each question and how you can best demonstrate those skills. Read through the following information. It will help you to understand how to answer each question.

Section A: Question 1

Example Exam Question

> **1 1** Read the article, 'Sailing Solo Across the Atlantic' by Max Campbell.
>
> **a)** How many miles did Max Campbell have left of his journey when the accident occurred? **[1 mark]**
>
> **b)** Name one thing that caught fire when the bottle of methylated spirit exploded. **[1 mark]**
>
> **c)** Which famous charity did Max Campbell previously work for? **[1 mark]**

You should spend about 3–4 minutes on these questions.

What is being tested?
- Your ability to identify explicit information. (AO1 1a)

What you have to do
- Identify the correct text.
- Read carefully to find specific details from across the whole passage to answer each of the questions.

Tips

- Check the mark tariff. Each part of Question 1 is usually worth one or two marks, so aim to spend no more than three or four minutes on this question.
- Track through the text chronologically – the answer to the first question is likely to appear before the others.
- Use skimming and scanning reading skills to identify the correct area of the text – this will help you to spot topic specific words.
- When you think you have found the answer, read the text surrounding it, to make sure you have the exact piece of information you need. For example, in question c, you need to identify which charity, not just the word, 'charity'.
- Only write down the key details that are required. For example, in Question 1b above, you only need to write down the name of one item (an item that caught on fire).
- Remember to only use information that is explicitly mentioned in the text.

Preparing to practise

Section A: Question 2

Example Exam Question

| 1 | 2 | How does Max Campbell try to show that his journey was dramatic?

You should comment on:

- what he says
- his use of language, tone and structure
- other ways that make his account sound dramatic

[10 marks]

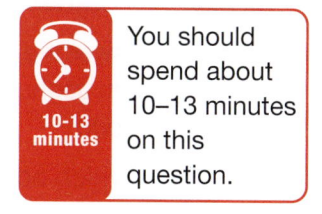

You should spend about 10–13 minutes on this question.

What is being tested?

- Your ability to explain, comment on and analyse how writers use language and structure to achieve effects and influence readers, using relevant subject terminology where appropriate. (AO2 1a, b, c and d)

What you have to do

- Read the whole passage.
- Write down a range of different details used by the writer to make the journey sound dramatic and exciting; this evidence will help you to support your answer.
- Think about *how* your chosen ideas/evidence make it sound exciting and dramatic.
- Where relevant, comment on the effect of the writer's tone, style, structure, and language, using relevant subject terminology.

Tips

- As you write, refer back to the question to make sure you remain on task and link your writing back to the phrasing of the question.
- Remember to explain *how* the journey is made to sound dramatic in the language, rather than just give examples from the text. Question 2 is assessing how you write about the effects of language.
- Only select evidence that is relevant to the focus of the question.
- Consider the tone of the passage that is created by the language used. For example, the phrase 'dark shapes creeping up from behind like a pack of wolves' creates a scary and dramatic tone, as the reader anticipates something negative could happen.
- Consider the way in which the passage is structured. Does the order of the information add to the drama?

113

Chapter 4: Component 2

Section A: Question 3

Example Exam Question

1 3	To answer the following questions you will need to read Captain Joshua Slocum's account of 'Sailing Alone Around the World'.
	a) In which ocean is Captain Joshua Slocum sailing? [1 mark]
	b) How far away was Port Angosto? [1 mark]
	c) How did Captain Joshua Slocum secure his boat when he reached Port Angosto? [1 mark]

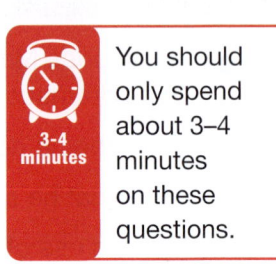

You should only spend about 3–4 minutes on these questions.

What is being tested?

- Your ability to identify and interpret explicit and implicit information and ideas. (AO1 1a, b, c and d)

What you have to do

- Look at the instruction above the questions. This tells you that you are now answering questions about a different text.
- Read the questions carefully and identify the correct information in the text.

Tips

- Work through the questions and text chronologically.
- Skim and scan the passage to help you quickly find the correct details. Look for the key words from the question and try to find them in the text.
- Always read the sentences surrounding your answer, so you can make sure you are reading in context.
- Copy down any information from the text carefully to avoid errors.
- Try to answer quickly and efficiently so you can save time for the longer, more demanding questions.
- Label your answers clearly (e.g. 3a, 3b, 3c).
- Remember that Question 3 may assess your skills in finding information that is implied, as well as explicitly stated in the text.

Section A: Question 4

Example Exam Question

| 1 | 4 | 'In this extract, Captain Joshua Slocum faces some difficult conditions.' How far do you agree with this view?

You should comment on:
- what he says
- how it is said

[10 marks]

You must refer to the text to support your comments.

You should spend about 10–13 minutes on this question.

What is being tested?
- Your ability to evaluate texts critically and support this with appropriate textual references (AO4)

What you have to do
- Read the whole passage and question carefully.
- Look for evidence that conveys the difficult conditions Slocum faces.
- Analyse the effects of your chosen evidence.
- Consider how the writer presents the difficulty of the conditions.
- Consider the extent to which you agree with the statement and support your view with details from the text.

Tips

- Remember to carefully read the bullet points of the question. It will tell you exactly what to include in your response.

- For this question, you have been asked to focus on the 'difficult conditions'. Try to find some synonyms in the text that could be used to describe something as difficult.

- Think carefully about *how* the writer presents the difficulty of the conditions. Focus on specific language, phrases and techniques, and evaluate the effects.

- As you write your response, reuse the words of the question and refer back to the question so you remain on task. For example, 'the extent of the difficulty of the conditions is highlighted through…'.

- Remember Question 4 is asking for your views. Make sure you include some personal comments and evaluations about the text and statement. Use these to help you decide how far you agree with the statement in the question and give reasons to support your answer.

115

Chapter 4: Component 2

Section A: Question 5

Example Exam Question

| 1 5 | To answer the following questions you must use both texts.

Using information from both texts, explain briefly in your own words how the two sailors reacted to the weather conditions.

[4 marks]

You should spend approximately 5–6 minutes on this question.

What is being tested?

- Your ability to select and synthesise evidence from different texts. (AO1 2a and b)

What you have to do

- Read the question carefully and work out the specific focus of the question.
- Refer to both texts. Find a couple of examples of evidence from each text to answer the question. You can link similar ideas together.
- Write your response clearly, including the relevant details that you have found in each text.

Tips

- For Question 5, start by working out the specific focus of the question: for example, how the sailors reacted to the weather conditions. Do not focus on anything else in your response.
- Be mindful of the time as this question is only worth four marks.
- To achieve the most marks, include more than one relevant detail from each text.
- Do not give reasons or detailed explanations; they are not required to answer this question.
- Question 5 is testing how well you select and synthesise evidence from two different texts. Therefore, where possible, try to answer in your own words to show your understanding.
- Quotations are acceptable but never copy large, unselective chunks directly from the text.
- Do not compare; this technique is not required to answer Question 5.

Section A: Question 6

Example Exam Question

| 1 | 6 | Both of these texts describe a solo yacht journey.

Compare:
- what Captain Joshua Slocum and Max Campbell did during their journeys
- how the writers try to convey the dangers of what they did

[10 marks]

You must use the text to support your comments and make it clear which text you are referring to.

You should spend about 10–13 minutes on this question.

What is being tested?
- Your ability to compare writers' ideas and perspectives, as well as how these are conveyed, across the two texts. (AO3 1a, b, c and d)

What you have to do
- Read the question carefully so you are able to detect if there is a specific focus.
- Note that the focus is what the sailors did during their journeys and how the dangers are conveyed, so select evidence from the texts to reflect this.
- Use both texts to answer the question.
- Consider the ways which both writers get across the dangers to the reader.
- Remember to make clear comparisons and contrasts about the two texts and the evidence you select.

Tips

- Question 6 is a comparison question; make sure you constantly focus on comparing the two texts.
- As far as possible, try to give a balanced number of points from each text.
- Always make it clear which text or writer you are referring to (and do this throughout your answer). Use the title of each text or the writer's surname explicitly in your response.
- Where possible, include comparative language to show that you are comparing the details, for example, 'Campbell highlights the danger of the weather by… whereas Slocum focuses on…'.
- Be specific rather than generalised: avoid making general statements like 'they both faced dangers' or 'both journeys had a lot of bad weather'.
- Give careful consideration to the second bullet and compare how the writers get across their feelings. For example, this could be through the language, the tone used or any personal opinions or observations they make.

Chapter 4: Component 2

Section B: Questions 1 and 2

In Section B of the paper, you have two writing tasks to complete.

Example Exam Question

> **2 1** This is part of an article that appeared in a newspaper:
>
> 'All young people should be encouraged to take a gap year or do something adventurous.'
>
> Write a letter to the newspaper giving your views on this subject.
>
> [20 marks]
>
> **2 2** Write a lively article for your school or college magazine with the heading:
>
> 'A healthy mind is just as important as a healthy body.'
>
> Write your article.
>
> [20 marks]

You should aim to spend:
- 5 minutes planning each task
- 25 minutes writing a response to each task

What is being tested?

- Your ability to communicate clearly, effectively and imaginatively, selecting and adapting tone, style and register for different forms, purposes and audiences. (AO5 1a, b, c)
- Your ability to organise information and ideas, using structural and grammatical features to support coherence and cohesion of texts. (AO5 2a, b, c)
- Your ability to use a range of vocabulary and sentence structures for clarity, purpose and effect, with accurate spelling and punctuation. (AO6)

What you have to do

- Always spend a few minutes planning a response for both tasks.
- Think about the format for your writing: task 1 is a formal letter and task 2 is a magazine article.
- Produce a clear and coherent piece of writing based on each task.
- Write in a suitable tone, style and register for the purpose and audience in the question.
- Structure your writing consciously and effectively and remember to use paragraphs.
- Present your viewpoint persuasively and convincingly.
- Link and develop a range of valid ideas, and use effective and carefully selected vocabulary.
- Use a range of effective technical devices/skills. For example, you might include some deliberate repetition, a rhetorical question, a series of facts and some imperative verbs.
- Write and punctuate your work accurately using a range of sentence structures.

Preparing to practise

Tips

- Focus on each writing task one at a time; you have 30 minutes (including five minutes planning) to spend on each question.
- Your writing in this question is being assessed based on the quality of your content and your ability to write accurately.
- For each task, plan what you are going to write before you begin and think carefully about how you will develop the level of detail in each paragraph.
- Look carefully for the audience and purpose of the writing in the question. How will you ensure your writing appeals to them?
- Both tasks require a personal opinion or view. Make sure that you communicate this clearly.
- Leave time at the end to proofread your response, and make corrections or improvements.

Activity 1 Answering the sample paper

Using all of the skills and techniques suggested on pages 112–119, complete the exam paper on pages 108–111.

Chapter 4: Component 2

Understanding the mark scheme

A mark scheme is used by examiners and teachers to assess the quality of your response for each question. Understanding the mark scheme can help you to improve the quality of your work as you will know what is needed to gain the highest marks in each question.

Section A: Question 1

Read the sample Question 1 below from the practice exam paper on pages 108–111.

Example Exam Question

> **1 1** Read the article, 'Sailing Solo Across the Atlantic' by Max Campbell.
>
> **a)** How many miles did Max Campbell have left of his journey when the accident occurred? **[1 mark]**
>
> **b)** Name one thing that caught fire when the bottle of methylated spirit exploded. **[1 mark]**
>
> **c)** Which famous charity did Max Campbell previously work for? **[1 mark]**

This question tests your ability to identify explicit information from a text (AO1 1a). You will be given this type of question for both texts in your Component 2 exam. There are three questions, each usually worth one mark.

Mark scheme

Below is the mark scheme for Question 1 of the sample exam paper. It is a list of indicative content.

> Award one mark for each correct response in a), b) and c).
> **a)** 200 miles (1)
> **b)** Award 1 mark to any **one** of the following:
>   - his duvet
>   - his clothing
>   - his own body (1)
> **c)** RNLI (1)

Improving your Section A: Question 1 response

Activity 2 Self-assessment

1. Look again at your original responses to Question 1. For this type of question, your answers need to exactly match those in the mark scheme. Refer to the mark scheme above and decide how many marks you would award yourself for your answers.

2. If any of your answers were incorrect, find the correct answer in the source text, circle it and rewrite your responses.

Understanding the mark scheme

> **Upgrade**
>
> - Remember it is not necessary for you to write down a lengthy response: this type of question should be answered quickly so you can move on to the more demanding higher mark questions.
> - Although these questions seem straightforward, many candidates lose marks because they do not read the source text closely enough. When you think you have found the correct answer in the text, read the paragraph or sentences around it, to make sure it is definitely correct.

Section A: Question 2

Read the sample Question 2 below from the practice exam paper on pages 108–111.

Example Exam Question

> **1 2** How does Max Campbell try to show that his journey was dramatic?
>
> You should comment on:
>
> - what he says
> - his use of language, tone and structure
> - other ways that make his account sound dramatic
>
> [10 marks]

This question tests your ability to explain, comment on and analyse how writers use language and structure to achieve effects and influence readers, using relevant subject terminology where appropriate (AO2 1a, b, c and d). Question 2 is assessed using marking bands: each band contains key words and phrases, which examiners use to decide the mark given to a response. These key words and the criteria for each band can be found in the table below.

Band	Marks	Key words/ phrases	Explanation
1	1–2 marks	'simply', 'brief', 'limited'	This means that you are beginning to make a few simple comments. Your response may be short and/or lacking in detail.
2	3–4 marks	'some', 'simple', 'limited'	This means that your response may include some straightforward comments and relevant details. Your coverage of the text may be limited.
3	5–6 marks	'commented', 'begin to show', 'range'	This means that you are able to make valid points about a range of examples. You begin to show how features such as words/phrases, tone and structure are used, and you are sometimes able to indicate when a relevant term has been used.
4	7–8 marks	'accurate', 'analyse', 'effectively', 'good range'	This means that you have made sensible and accurate comments about a good range of different examples. You analyse how areas such as language, tone and structure are used to influence the reader. You use subject terminology to support your comments.
5	9–10 marks	'accurate', 'perceptive', 'wide range'	This means that you have made accurate and perceptive comments about a wide range of different examples. Your response provides detailed analysis. You accurately use relevant subject terminology to support your comments.

Chapter 4: Component 2

Mark scheme

Below is the mark scheme for the sample Question 2 from the practice paper. The key words from each band have been highlighted to help you see how the skills level increases, as progress is made through the bands.

Band 1	Give 1–2 marks to those who simply identify a few textual details to show that the journey was dramatic. These responses are likely to be brief and limited.
Band 2	Give 3–4 marks to those who identify some of the textual details that show the journey was dramatic. These responses may include some simple comments alongside some relevant selection of detail, although coverage and comments across the whole text may be limited. These responses may simply identify some subject terminology.
Band 3	Give 5–6 marks to those who have identified and commented on a range of examples that Max Campbell uses in the text to show why/how the journey was dramatic. These responses begin to show how aspects such as language, tone and structure are used to achieve effects and influence the reader. These responses may begin to use relevant subject terminology to support their comments, where appropriate.
Band 4	Give 7–8 marks to those who have made accurate comments about a good range of different examples that Max Campbell uses in the text to show why/how the journey was dramatic. These responses begin to analyse how aspects such as language, tone and structure are used to influence the reader. Relevant subject terminology is used to support comments effectively, where appropriate.
Band 5	Give 9–10 marks to those who have made accurate and perceptive comments about a wide range of different examples that Max Campbell uses in the text to show why/how the journey was dramatic. These responses will provide detailed analysis of how aspects such as language, tone and structure are used to achieve effects and influence readers. Well-considered, accurate use of relevant subject terminology supports comments effectively where appropriate.

The mark scheme also includes a list of indicative content. This provides suggested examples of the content that you may include as part of a successful answer to Question 2. This is not a complete list, but is a good indicator of the most relevant content for the answer. Below is the indicative content list for the sample Question 2.

Details candidates may explore or comment on could be:

- it is dramatic that he completed this event alone at the age of 21: 'single-handed'
- immediate contrast in weather shows the changing and challenging nature of the journey
- he describes the weather conditions as 'unfamiliar', suggesting he is not prepared
- he describes the squalls 'like a pack of wolves', suggesting the weather can be aggressive/violent
- he has near misses: 'catching me off guard'
- he recognises the highs and lows: 'on top of the world', 'punish me with fury', and the constant contrast makes it particularly dramatic
- the accident is described using words like 'exploded', 'ravaged' – very dramatic language use
- we realise that the accident could have been much worse – drama is created as he is alone
- the description of his injuries is dramatic
- he has to treat himself (he has no other option but to do so)
- in hospital he lies in bed 'dressed like a mummy' showing the severity of the injuries
- he still loves adventure and had 'seven amazing months'
- the language used is exaggerated: 'incredible', 'euphoric', 'grasping for my life'

Understanding the mark scheme

- the comparisons between the weather and his emotions throughout the text, to reflect the turbulence of the journey
- sentence lengths are varied to add pace and drama, and to mimic the changes in activity and drama throughout the passage

This is not a checklist and the question must be marked in levels of response. Look for and reward valid alternatives.

Tip

When you are asked to consider how something is dramatic, there are many things that you can focus on. Drama is an exciting, emotional, or unexpected/tense event or circumstance. It is important to remember that something dramatic can be both positive and/or negative but it will be something out of the ordinary.

Sample student responses

Below are extracts from two different answers to this question. The first extract is taken from an answer that was given a mark in Band 2 and the second extract is taken from an answer that was given a mark in Band 4.

Student A

The journey was dramatic because Max was in 'unfamiliar conditions'. The journey is also dramatic as things go wrong for example, the 'sails and poles came crashing down to the deck'. Another way that it is dramatic is that he has an accident and is 'covered in flames'. The final way that it is dramatic is because the weather changes all the time, for example a 'heavy downpour'.

Student B

This dramatic passage has challenging weather as in '…an increase in wind and a heavy downpour'. The conditions are beyond his previous experience, which we find out when he says he struggled: 'In the unfamiliar conditions, I struggled'. This creates drama as he may not be equipped to deal with it. He describes the squalls (or storms) as 'dark shapes creeping up from behind like a pack of wolves', suggesting the weather is aggressive and threatening. The text picks up pace, as things become damaged on the boat, for example: 'sails and poles came crashing down to the deck', which creates drama as the reader is unsure if he can survive the damage. When the accident occurs in 'a flaming bottle of methylated spirit exploded in my hand', the verb 'exploded' sounds uncontrolled and life threatening. The resulting injuries are graphically described to emphasise the severe damage, for example: 'Charred pieces of skin fell off my arms, chest, and torso'. This is dramatic as we are aware that it could have been worse. The anticlimax at the end is an unexpected way to end and drama is created through the language, such as, 'I felt completely robbed of celebration', suggesting he has been cheated out of his victory.

Chapter 4: Component 2

Activity 3 Building levels of response

1. Look at the two sample answers. Student A was awarded a Band 2 mark for the answer and Student B's answer is part of a Band 4 response. What do you think the key differences are between these two answers? For example, look at the evidence that has been selected and the level of detail provided.

2. Look again at the mark scheme for this question and focus on Band 5. How could you improve the Band 4 answer to achieve a Band 5 mark? Complete the following annotations:

    a. Underline the range of different examples that have been included.

    b. Circle the insightful comments that have been made about those examples.

    c. Highlight any use of subject terminology to explore tone, language or structure.

3. Select two sentences from the Band 4 answer on page 123. Consider the things you have noticed in your annotations and refer back to the mark scheme on page 122, and then rewrite those sentences to move this answer from Band 4 to Band 5.

Improving your Section A: Question 2 response

Activity 4 Self-assessment

1. Look at your original response to Question 2. Decide which band your response best matches. Use the mark scheme and indicative content on pages 122–123 and the two sample answers to help you make your decision.

2. Think about which parts of your response you could develop in order to improve it. Look at the quality of what you have written, paying close attention to the comments you have made about your selected evidence.

    a. Have you commented on the tone, structure or language in the evidence selected?

    b. Do you understand what 'dramatic' means?

    c. Did your answer cover details from across the whole passage? Do you consistently refer to the question?

    d. Have you linked your ideas so that the whole response sounds fluent?

3. Rewrite your response, paying particular attention to the areas you have identified above that could be developed or improved. Check your revised answer against the mark scheme to see if it would now achieve a higher mark.

Upgrade

- Consider adding an overview sentence to summarise the key points of why the passage is dramatic.
- Consider the structure of the text in your response. Think about the sequence of information and how this adds to the drama.

Understanding the mark scheme

Section A: Question 3

Read the sample Question 3 below from the practice exam paper on pages 108–111.

Example Exam Question

1 3 To answer the following question you will need to read Captain Joshua Slocum's account of 'Sailing Alone Around the World'.

a) In which ocean is Captain Joshua Slocum sailing? [1 mark]

b) How far away was Port Angosto? [1 mark]

c) How did Captain Joshua Slocum secure his boat when he reached Port Angosto? [1 mark]

Question 3, like Question 1, tests your ability to retrieve information from a text (AO1 1a, b, c and d). The instruction before the question informs you that you are now working on a different text.

For Question 3, you are awarded one mark for each correct answer, up to a total of three marks.

Mark scheme

Below is the mark scheme for the sample Question 3 from the practice paper. It is a list of indicative content.

Award one mark for each correct response:

a) The Pacific Ocean (1)   b) 26 miles (1)

c) (two anchors) by cables to trees (1)

Improving your Section A: Question 3 response

Activity 5 Self-assessment

1. Look again at your original responses to Question 3. For this type of question, your answers need to exactly match those in the mark scheme. Refer to the mark scheme above and decide how many marks you would award yourself for your answers.

2. If any of your answers were incorrect, find the correct answer in the source text, circle it and rewrite your responses.

Upgrade

- When writing down your answers, the marks are awarded for the correct details. You are not given extra credit for writing in sentences, so a numbered list of each answer is perfectly acceptable to save time.

- As with Question 1, once you find the correct answer in the text, make sure that you read the text surrounding it to make sure it definitely makes sense in response to the question.

125

Chapter 4: Component 2

Section A: Question 4

Read the sample Question 4 below from the practice exam paper on pages 108–111.

> **Example Exam Question**
>
> **1 4** 'In this extract, Captain Joshua Slocum faces some difficult conditions.' How far do you agree with this view?
>
> You should comment on:
>
> - what he says
> - how it is said **[10 marks]**
>
> *You must refer to the text to support your comments.*

This question tests your ability to evaluate texts critically and support this with appropriate textual references (AO4). Question 4 also requires a personal response alongside analysis of the text.

Question 4, like Question 2, is assessed using marking bands: each band contains key words and phrases, which examiners use to decide the mark given to a response. These key words and the criteria for each band can be found in the table below.

Band	Marks	Key words/phrases	Explanation
1	1–2 marks	'brief', 'limited', 'some basic textual details'	This means that you are beginning to make some simple and straightforward comments and can back this up with some basic references to the text. Your response may be short and/or lacking in detail.
2	3–4 marks	'a few relevant details', 'a personal response'	This means that your response may include some simple comments and pick out a few relevant details from the text. Your coverage of the text may be limited.
3	5–6 marks	'evaluation', 'a range of relevant details', 'personal response'	This means that you are able to identify and comment on a range of examples. You begin to show how areas such as language, tone and structure are used. Your response may begin to use relevant subject terminology.
4	7–8 marks	'critical evaluation', 'a good range of well-selected details', 'understanding'	This means that you have made sensible and accurate comments about a good range of different examples. You analyse how areas such as language, tone and structure are used to influence the reader. You use subject terminology to support your comments.
5	9–10 marks	'detailed and persuasive evaluation', 'convincing, well-selected examples', 'purposeful', 'engagement', 'involvement', 'perceptive'	This means that you have made accurate and perceptive comments about a wide range of different examples across the whole text. Your response provides detailed analysis. You accurately use relevant subject terminology to support your comments.

Understanding the mark scheme

Mark scheme

Below is the mark scheme for the sample Question 4 from the practice paper. The key words from each band have been highlighted to help you see how the level of skill required increases, as progress is made through the bands.

Band 1	Give 1-2 marks to those who select some basic textual details and/or express a simple personal opinion. Responses in this band may be brief and limited and /or struggle to engage with the text or the question.
Band 2	Give 3-4 marks to those who select a few relevant details from the text and/or give a personal response to Slocum's account, although coverage of the whole text may be limited.
Band 3	Give 5-6 marks to those who give an evaluation of the text supported by a range of relevant details from across the text. These responses will show some critical awareness and exploration of Slocum's account that inform a personal response.
Band 4	Give 7-8 marks to those who give a detailed, critical evaluation of the text and its effects, supported by a good range of well-selected details from across the text. Personal response comments will be linked to a critical awareness and understanding of Slocum's account.
Band 5	Give 9-10 marks to those who give a detailed and persuasive evaluation of the text and its effects, supported by convincing, well-selected examples and purposeful textual references. These responses will show engagement and involvement, where candidates take an overview to make perceptive comments and evaluation of Slocum's account.

The mark scheme also includes a list of indicative content. This provides suggested examples of the content that you may include as part of a successful answer to Question 4. This is not a complete list, but is a good indicator of the most relevant content for the answer. Below is the indicative content list for the sample Question 4.

Details that candidates may evaluate or give a personal response to could be:

- the weather conditions are changing and challenging: a snowstorm would restrict his view
- the wind is also a challenge, especially given the intensity of the gusts: 'gale'
- the promise of 'safe harbour' creates a contrast to the challenges at sea
- 'Between the storm-bursts' suggests that his vision is impaired by the weather
- 'steering for it when…' 'a sudden blast of wind' constant contrasts of hope and challenge
- 'nearly … the cause of disaster' suggests the constant threat that he faces
- the weather is impairing his vision and nightfall intensifies the challenge: 'close upon night'
- 'I worked till the perspiration poured from my body' suggests that repairing the damage is a physical challenge
- 'Even then I did not get the boom shipped in its saddle' suggests that despite effort, he is unable to repair it fully
- the simile 'like a bird with a broken wing' highlights the potential for disaster
- the word 'jeopardised' suggests there is a very real potential for disaster – he is constantly under pressure
- even securing the boat isn't straightforward and requires two anchors and cables tied to trees

This is not a checklist and the question must be marked in levels of response. Look for and reward valid alternatives.

Chapter 4: Component 2

Sample student responses

Below are extracts from two different answers to this question. The first extract is taken from an answer that was given a mark in Band 3 and the second extract is taken from an answer that was given a mark in Band 5.

Student A

I agree Slocum faced difficult challenges but he never loses control. Firstly, 'I had only twenty-six miles to run' illustrates he is near his destination so we think it won't be too much of a problem to get there. The boat is described using the simile, 'she looked like a white winter bird', which while it is not negative, it suggests that the boat is coated in snow and therefore more difficult to sail. When the equipment fails, we see a challenge as 'the perspiration poured from my body'. This shows the writer is sweating despite the cold weather highlighting a very challenging and difficult situation. Overall, I agree that he faced some difficult conditions.

Student B

Slocum faces extreme weather conditions, which cause his yacht's malfunction and risk navigating the boat safely to refuge. In an unsettling contrast, Slocum conveys optimism with the weather conditions initially: 'another gale had then sprung up, but the wind was still fair'. Tension is created by the imminent nightfall as in, 'I carried on sailing to make the harbour before dark'. The idea of being close, yet far, to his destination reinforces this tension, as he only catches glimpses of the harbour through the storm, for example: 'Between the storm-bursts I saw the headland of my port' and possessive pronoun 'my' directly links the impact of not returning home back to Slocum. The weather continues to pose problems: 'a sudden blast of wind caught the mainsail'. The yacht is described with personification as 'she fairly flew along, all covered with snow, which fell thick and fast', which suggests 'she' required a human strength to fight the storm. Overall, the tone of the passage is pragmatic and experienced, but I agree that there is a constant underlying tension and threat to Slocum.

Activity 6 Building levels of response

1. Look at the two sample answers. Student A was awarded a Band 3 mark for the answer and Student B's answer is part of a Band 5 response. What are the key differences between the sample answers? Complete the following:

    a. Underline where students have included evidence from the text.

    b. Highlight where the student has commented on the writer's ideas.

    c. Circle where the student has commented on the writer's methods.

2. Look again at the Band 5 response above. Select a piece of indicative content from the mark scheme. Write a section of analysis in the same style as the Band 5 answer.

Improving your Section A: Question 4 response

Activity 7 Self-assessment

1. Look again at your original response to Question 4. Refer to the two sample answers, and the mark scheme and indicative content on page 127, and decide which mark you think your response would be awarded.

2. Think about which parts of your response you could develop in order to improve it. Consider the following:

    a. Have you made it clear how far you agree that the writer faces difficult conditions?

    b. Have you considered how the tone varies throughout the whole text? It is not constantly frenzied and difficult. What effect does this have on the reader?

    c. Have you commented on how the pace and tone develops through the text? How does the writer make it seem like he is constantly being challenged?

    d. Have you carefully explored the language that the writer uses? The writer is clearly an experienced sailor. Because of this, think about how the reader might see the dangers he faces.

    e. Have you used synonyms for the word 'difficult', such as 'tough', 'arduous', 'gruelling', 'strenuous' and 'relentless', to avoid repetition in your answer?

3. Rewrite your response, paying particular attention to the areas you have identified above that could be developed or improved, and considering the Upgrade panel. Check your revised answer against the mark scheme to see if it would now achieve a higher mark.

Upgrade

- Remember to link your ideas together to build a coherent, persuasive answer. Look at the table on page 93 for language that you could use to make links between points.
- Constantly probe why certain words and phrases have been used; these are deliberate decisions made by the writer to achieve effects.

Chapter 4: Component 2

Section A: Question 5

Read the sample Question 5 below from the practice exam paper on pages 108–111.

> **Example Exam Question**
>
> **1 5** To answer the following questions you must use both texts.
>
> Using information from both texts, explain briefly in your own words how the two sailors reacted to the weather conditions.
>
> **[4 marks]**

This question tests your ability to select and synthesise evidence from both texts (AO1 2a and b). You need to use a few details or ideas from each text to answer the question. Because this question is worth four marks, there are only four marking bands so a table to analyse the mark scheme has not been included.

Mark scheme

Below is the mark scheme for the sample Question 5 from the practice paper. Some key words from each band have been highlighted to help you see how the skills level increases, as progress is made through the bands.

Band 1	Give 1 mark to those who **struggle** to offer a relevant detail from each of the texts or **offer relevant detail from just one** text.
Band 2	Give 2 marks to those who select **at least a relevant detail** from each of the texts.
Band 3	Give 3 marks to those who select **relevant details** from both texts.
Band 4	Give 4 marks to those who synthesise with **clear understanding** and provide an **overview** drawn from a **range of relevant details** from both texts.

The mark scheme also includes a list of indicative content. This provides suggested examples of the content that you may include as part of a successful answer to Question 5. This is not a complete list, but is a good indicator of the most relevant content for the answer. Below is the indicative content list for the sample Question 5.

> Details that candidates may select, explore or respond to could be:
>
> - **Both focus on the constantly and rapidly changing weather conditions and the extent to which these can influence the sailing experience.**
>
> | Campbell: | Slocum: |
> |---|---|
> | • observant and descriptive in noticing the weather: 'I noticed a few grey clouds' | • accepts the weather and is quite relaxed: 'the wind was still fair' |
> | • accepting of the weather he faces | • positive reaction in the face of snow: 'flew along, all covered with snow' |
> | • sees the struggle of sailing during turbulent weather: 'increase in wind and a heavy downpour' | • almost sees the positives in the weather: 'she looked like a white winter bird' |
> | • recognises that you can't prepare for every weather condition: 'unfamiliar' conditions | • pragmatic when facing a storm: 'Between the storm-bursts I saw the headland of my port' |

130

Understanding the mark scheme

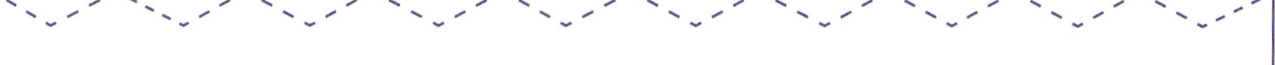

- reactive to weather and sees the importance of being ready for it: 'I would jump out of the cabin'
- recognises the damage it can cause, 'a sudden blast of wind caught the mainsail', but is practical and seeks to resolve any problems

This is not a checklist and the question must be marked in levels of response. Look for and reward valid alternatives.

Sample student answer

Below is an extract from a sample answer to this question. This extract was taken from an answer that was given a mark in Band 4.

Although the texts were written over one hundred years apart, both sailors have a pragmatic approach to the weather and are relatively calm in accepting the challenges that it poses. Campbell shows awareness of the changing conditions, for example 'I noticed a few grey clouds' and 'increase in wind and a heavy downpour'. He also recognises the direct link between the weather and his experience – sailing is more difficult when the weather is tough. Campbell reacts to the weather he faces by tackling the challenges head on, for example 'I would jump out of the cabin'. Like Campbell, Slocum accepts the weather and is quite relaxed, saying 'the wind was still fair'. Even in the face of adverse weather conditions, such as snow, he is positive in his outlook, saying the boat simply 'flew along, all covered with snow'. Slocum's yacht is damaged by the weather conditions he faces but he is pragmatic and works hard, causing 'perspiration', to resolve the damage.

Overall, both react to the weather with a calm resilience. They know that the weather is beyond their control and so they seek to limit the effects it can have on them.

Activity 8 Building levels of response

1. Band 2 candidates 'select' a relevant detail from each text. Look closely at the bands. What is the main difference between Band 2 and Band 3?

2. Student A's response was marked in Band 4 (remember that this is the top band for this question). Using the Band 4 criteria, annotate the response and see if you can work out where and why they were awarded four marks.

    a. Underline where it shows clear understanding of the text.

    b. Circle an overview point that has been included.

    c. Highlight the range in relevant details that has been included from both texts.

    d. Compare Student A's response to the response you produced. What are the differences between your own answer and the sample answer?

Chapter 4: Component 2

Improving your Section A: Question 5 response

Activity 9 Self-assessment

1. Look again at your original response to Question 5. Refer to the Band 4 sample answer, and the mark scheme and indicative content on pages 130–131, and decide which mark you think your response would be awarded.

2. Think about which parts of your response you could develop in order to improve it. Look in particular at the quality of what you have written about each individual text.

   a. Have you included a similar level of evidence and detail about each text? Is the evidence you have selected relevant to the question?

   b. Look again at the indicative content and choose one additional area that you could add for each text.

   c. Have you focused clearly on the reactions of both sailors?

   d. Have you attempted to include a brief overview to show your overall understanding of the texts and the question? Consider the advice in the upgrade panel.

3. Rewrite your response, paying particular attention to the areas you have identified above that could be developed or improved. Check your revised answer against the mark scheme to see if it would now achieve a higher mark.

Upgrade

- Remind yourself of the definition of synthesise: to bring together information from different sources to create a new text. Make sure you comment on both texts: cover them in the same level of detail and make it clear which text you got the information from.
- Make sure your answer clearly focuses on the purpose of the question by referring back to the phrasing of it throughout your answer.

Understanding the mark scheme

Section A: Question 6

Read the sample Question 6 below from the practice exam paper on pages 108–111.

> **Example Exam Question**
>
> **1 6** Both of these texts describe a solo yacht journey.
>
> Compare:
>
> - what Captain Joshua Slocum and Max Campbell did during their journeys
> - how the writers try to convey the dangers of what they did
>
> **[10 marks]**
>
> *You must use the text to support your comments and make it clear which text you are referring to.*

This question tests your ability to compare writers' ideas and perspectives, as well as how these are conveyed, across the two texts in your exam paper (AO3). Question 6 is assessed using marking bands: each band contains key words and phrases, which examiners use to decide the mark given to a response. These key words and the criteria for each band can be found in the table below.

Band	Marks	Key words/phrases	Explanation
1	1–2 marks	'basic similarity and/or difference', 'not clear'	This means that you may not make it clear which text is being referred to. You will have limited focus and may make limited comparisons.
2	3–4 marks	'some similarities and differences', 'some evidence', 'some focus'	This means that you use some evidence to make some comparisons. You might attempt to comment on how the writers get across their ideas.
3	5–6 marks	'similarities and differences', 'appropriate comments'	This means that you find features to compare and contrast both texts and make some relevant comments on how the writers get across their experiences.
4	7–8 marks	'detailed comparisons', 'range of valid comments'	This means that you explain comparisons and analyse how the writers get across their experiences.
5	9–10 marks	'comparisons are sustained and detailed', 'clear understanding', 'wide range'	This means that you make detailed comparisons throughout your answer and go on to show a clear understanding of the different ways in which the writers get across their experiences through lots of different valid comments.

Chapter 4: Component 2

Mark scheme

Below is the mark scheme for the sample Question 6 from the practice paper. The key words from each band have been highlighted to help you see how the skills level increases, as progress is made through the bands.

Band 1	Give 1-2 marks to those who identify a basic similarity and/or difference in what the texts say about what the sailors did during their journeys. Marks in this band may only deal with one text or not make it clear to which text is being referred.
Band 2	Give 3-4 marks to those who identify and give a straightforward description of some similarities and differences in what the texts say about what the sailors did during their journeys. Some evidence will be used to support ideas and comparisons. Some focus on how the writers get across their ideas may be emerging.
Band 3	Give 5-6 marks to those who identify similarities and differences in what the texts say about what the sailors did during their journeys and make some appropriate comments on how the writers get across their experiences to their readers.
Band 4	Give 7-8 marks to those who make detailed comparisons about what the sailors did during their journeys and offer a range of valid comments about how the writers get across their experiences to their readers.
Band 5	Give 9-10 marks to those who make comparisons that are sustained and detailed about what the sailors did during their journeys and go on to show a clear understanding of the different ways in which the writers get across their experiences to their readers through a wide range of valid comments.

The mark scheme also includes a list of indicative content. This provides suggested examples of the content that you may include as part of a successful answer to Question 6. This is not a complete list, but is a good indicator of the most relevant content for the answer. Below is the indicative content list for the sample Question 6.

Details that candidates may explore or comment on could be:

1. What the writers did

Campbell:
- worked to maintain the safety of yacht: 'remove the pole… lash down one of the sails'
- constantly on guard: 'jump out of the cabin'
- constantly developing skills/experience: 'lesson well and truly learned'
- faced a serious accident – explosion of 'paraffin stove' – has to extinguish fire
- uses his first aid skills: 'having to treat myself'

Slocum:
- maintaining the set course and constantly battling with the weather conditions
- faces very challenging weather conditions: 'nearly was this the cause of disaster'
- worked hard to repair the yacht: 'perspiration'
- constantly challenged: 'I was at the entrance of the harbour before I could get this done'
- manoeuvres his yacht with expertise and takes time to ensure it has been secured properly

Understanding the mark scheme

2. How they get across their experiences to their readers:		
Campbell:	**Slocum:**	**Both:**
• language used indicates the constant element of danger/threat to this journey	• like Campbell, Slocum repeatedly refers to the adverse/changing weather conditions	• dramatic language choices highlight the highs and lows of the journeys
• contrast of the weather emphasises the difficulty of what he did	• the pace of the passage is rapid to reflect the frenetic nature of the journey	• constant references to the changing weather show the tumultuous nature of the journeys
• he is constantly busy, which is reflected in the pace of the passage	• the language highlights the vulnerable position he is in: 'nearly the cause of disaster'	• the passages are full of references to challenge and difficulty
• structurally, we are presented with ups and downs and contrasts to mirror his experiences	• there is danger in the equipment – 'treacherous fiber' – and this language is emotive and extreme	
• 'struggled' is repeated to show the constant challenges he faces	• we are told he has to be cautious: 'doubly sure'	
• at the end, we are told he travelled '5,000 miles', which suggests the enormity of the challenge		

This is not a checklist and the question must be marked in levels of response. Look for and reward valid alternatives.

Sample student answers

Below are extracts from two different answers to this question. The first extract is taken from an answer that was given a mark in Band 2 and the second extract is taken from an answer that was given a mark in Band 5.

Student A

Both of the writers had a lot to do on their boats, especially fixing them up after the bad weather. We can see that Campbell can't get a rest as he 'jumped out of the cabin' to fix the boat and Slocum was the same as he had to work so hard it caused 'perspiration'. They both convey dangers and responsibilities because they tell you exactly what it is like and tell you what is hard.

Student B

Campbell informs the reader that the journey poses constant challenges that he is not always prepared for, such as 'one squall succeeded in catching me off guard'. He doesn't always get everything right and has to repair the damage caused. Slocum also focuses on the complications caused by the weather, for example, 'the sheet parted and a pole unshipped'; it would appear that this is unavoidable and, like Campbell, he has to deal with the consequences. The writers both get across the dangers by highlighting the ease with which these problems occur and the technical language used emphasises the fact that skill is required to repair the damage.

Chapter 4: Component 2

Activity 10 Building levels of response

1. Look at the two sample answers. Student A was awarded a Band 2 mark for the answer and Student B's answer is part of a Band 5 response. What are the key differences between these answers? Complete the following:

   a. Underline effective comparisons between the texts.

   b. Circle where textual references have been included.

   c. Highlight how textual references have been analysed for effects.

   d. Tick the words or phrases that make it clear which text the student is referring to.

2. Select a piece of indicative content from the list on pages 134–135. Follow the steps below to help you build a response to compare this in the two texts.

   a. Write down a sentence to compare or contrast this idea between the two source texts.

   b. Find some evidence in the both texts to support the point you have selected.

   c. Analyse this evidence and comment on how the information is conveyed, including any relevant subject terminology.

Improving your Section A: Question 6 response

Activity 11 Self-assessment

1. Look again at your original response to Question 6. Compare it to the Band 2 and Band 5 sample answers and the mark scheme and indicative content on pages 134–135. Decide which mark your response would be given.

2. Think about which parts of your response you could improve. Look in particular at the quality of what you have written about the individual texts.

   a. Have you remained focused on the comparison of the question?

   b. Have you given a balanced answer, focusing on each of the texts equally?

   c. Is there sufficient comparison in your answer?

   d. Have you included a range of points, rather than focusing on just one?

   e. Have you explored each point in detail and included evidence?

3. Rewrite your response, paying attention to the areas you identified above. Check your revised answer against the mark scheme to see if it would now achieve a higher mark.

Upgrade

- Remember to think about the writer's methods: how they put the information together and what techniques and language choices they used.
- Remember this is a comparative task. Use language to compare and contrast in your answer.

Understanding the mark scheme

Section B: Questions 1 and 2

Read the sample Question 1 and Question 2 below from Section B of the practice exam paper on pages 108–111.

> **Example Exam Question**
>
> **2 1**   This is part of an article that appeared in a newspaper:
>
> 'All young people should be encouraged to take a gap year or do something adventurous.'
>
> Write a letter to the newspaper giving your views on this subject.
>
> **[20 marks]**
>
> **2 2**   Write a lively article for your school or college magazine with the heading:
>
> 'A healthy mind is just as important as a healthy body.'
>
> Write your article.
>
> **[20 marks]**

These questions test your ability to:

- communicate clearly, effectively and imaginatively, selecting and adapting tone, style and register for different forms, purposes and audiences (AO5)
- organise information and ideas, using structural and grammatical features to support coherence and cohesion of texts (AO5)
- use a range of vocabulary and sentence structures for clarity, purpose and effect, with accurate spelling and punctuation (AO6).

Question 1 and 2 in Section B of the Component 2 exam paper are worth 20 marks each.

The mark scheme is divided into two sections to reflect the two assessment objectives. Of the 20 marks available for each writing question, the quality of your communication and organisation (AO5) is worth 12 marks for each task, and the quality of your vocabulary, sentence structure, spelling and punctuation (AO6) is worth eight marks for each task.

> **Tip**
>
> Unlike in Component 1, *both* writing tasks must be completed in Component 2. You have approximately one hour to complete both writing tasks, so you should aim to spend 5 minutes planning and 25 minutes writing each response.

Chapter 4: Component 2

Communication and Organisation (AO5)

The mark scheme for Communication and Organisation (AO5) is divided into marking bands: each band contains key words and phrases, which examiners use to decide the mark given to a response. These key words and the criteria for each band can be found in the table below.

Band	Key words/phrases	Explanation
1	'basic awareness', 'content may be thin and brief'	This means that your writing is quite simple and is not always organised in a way that makes sense. You may make some points clearly. Your reader struggles to follow what you have written and meaning is hindered by the inaccuracy of the writing. Your writing may be brief and undeveloped.
2	'awareness', 'limited development', 'some sequencing', 'fluency'	This means that your writing is sometimes clear and sometimes makes sense. Your writing is sometimes organised and some ideas are developed sensibly. You have tried to be clear in the way you put across your ideas but may not always be successful. Sometimes the reader may struggle to understand or lose the sense of your points/ideas.
3	'clear understanding', 'appropriately adapted', 'communication has clarity', 'fluency'	This means that your writing is mostly clear with appropriate reasons. You organise your writing with a sense of purpose and your writing is coherent. These answers will include a range of sensible details and will be clear. The writing will be mostly fluent and will interest a reader. There will be a clear awareness of the intended reader throughout.
4	'consistent understanding', 'secure awareness', 'well-judged and detailed', 'coherently developed'	This means that your writing is consistent, clear and well-judged. You organise your writing with clarity and you use language carefully to communicate your ideas. Your ideas are coherently developed, effective and relevant to the task. You have a secure awareness of your reader.
5	'sophisticated', 'sustained', 'confidently', 'ambitious, pertinent', 'convincingly developed'	This means that your writing has been crafted with confidence and ambition. You structure writing effectively and are willing to be ambitious and sophisticated in your use of language and ideas. You are able to fully engage your reader and develop your ideas with convincing details.

Below, and opposite, is the mark scheme for Communication and Organisation (AO5) for Section B: Questions 1 and 2 from the practice paper on pages 108–111. The key words from each band have been highlighted to help you see how the skills level increases, as progress is made through the bands.

Band 1	**1–2 marks** • basic awareness of the purpose and format of the task • some basic awareness of the reader/intended audience • some attempt to adapt register to purpose/audience • some relevant content despite uneven coverage of the topic • content may be thin and brief • simple sequencing of ideas (paragraphs may be used to show obvious divisions or group ideas into some order) • there is some basic clarity but communication of meaning is limited
Band 2	**3–4 marks** • shows some understanding of the purpose and format of the task • shows awareness of the reader/intended audience • a clear attempt to adapt register to purpose/audience • some reasons are given in support of opinions/ideas • limited development of ideas • some sequencing of ideas into paragraphs (structure/direction may be uncertain) • communication has some clarity and fluency

Understanding the mark scheme

Band 3	**5–7 marks** • shows clear understanding of the purpose and format of the task • shows clear awareness of the reader/intended audience • register is appropriately adapted to purpose/audience • content is developed, and appropriate reasons are given in support of opinions/ideas • ideas are organised into coherent arguments • there is some shape and structure in the writing (paragraphs are used to give sequence and organisation) • communication has clarity and fluency
Band 4	**8–10 marks** • shows consistent understanding of the purpose and format of the task • shows secure awareness of the reader/intended audience • register is appropriately and consistently adapted to purpose/audience • content is well-judged and detailed • ideas are organised and coherently developed with supporting detail • there is clear shape and structure in the writing (paragraphs are used effectively to give sequence and organisation) • communication has clarity, fluency and some ambition
Band 5	**11–12 marks** • shows sophisticated understanding of the purpose and format of the task • shows sustained awareness of the reader/intended audience • appropriate register is confidently adapted to purpose/audience • content is ambitious, pertinent and sophisticated • ideas are convincingly developed and supported by a range of relevant details • there is sophistication in the shape and structure of the writing • communication has ambition and sophistication

Vocabulary, Sentence structure, Spelling and Punctuation (AO6)

The mark scheme for Vocabulary, Sentence structure, Spelling and Punctuation (AO6) is also divided into five marking bands: each band contains key words and phrases, which examiners use to decide the mark given to a response. These key words and the criteria for each band can be found in the table below.

Band	Key words/phrases	Explanation
1	'limited range', 'control', 'some attempt'	This means that your writing is not very accurate. Your spelling and use of punctuation and grammar contain basic errors that hinder the meaning and/or your sentences lack variety. If you were to underline all of the errors in your work there would probably be a lot of areas underlined in your writing.
2	'some variety', 'control', 'usually accurate', 'generally secure', 'some range'	This means that your writing is sometimes accurate. Spelling, punctuation and grammar are sometimes controlled but there will be increasing errors across multiple areas (e.g. spelling, grammar and punctuation). Your use of vocabulary shows some range but this may be simple and/or have mixed success.
3	'variety in sentence structure', 'mostly secure', 'accurately', 'beginning to develop'	This means that your writing is mostly accurate and reliable. Spelling, punctuation and grammar are mostly controlled. Your use of vocabulary is beginning to show care and some thought.
4	'varied', 'secure', 'range used'	This means that your writing is generally very accurate and reliable. Spelling, punctuation and grammar are accurate and care has been taken. Your use of vocabulary is careful and thoughtful.
5	'appropriate and effective variation', 'controlled and accurate', 'confidently', 'totally secure', 'wide range', 'ambitious'	This means that your writing is extremely accurate. Errors rarely occur and your writing is technically sophisticated and carefully crafted for effect. You can use a wide range of carefully chosen vocabulary for maximum effect.

Chapter 4: Component 2

Below is the mark scheme for Vocabulary, Sentence structure, Spelling and Punctuation (AO6) for Section B: Questions 1 and 2 from the practice paper on pages 108–111. The key words from each band have been highlighted to help you see how the skills level increases, as progress is made through the bands.

Band 1	**1 mark** • ==limited range== of sentence structure • ==control== of sentence construction is limited • there is ==some attempt== to use punctuation • some spelling is accurate • control of tense and agreement is ==limited== • ==limited range== of vocabulary
Band 2	**2–3 marks** • ==some variety== of sentence structure • there is some ==control== of sentence construction • some control of a range of punctuation • the spelling is ==usually accurate== • control of tense and agreement is ==generally secure== • there is ==some range== of vocabulary
Band 3	**4–5 marks** • there is ==variety in sentence structure== • control of sentence construction is ==mostly secure== • a range of punctuation is used, mostly ==accurately== • most spelling, including that of irregular words, is correct • control of tense and agreement is mostly secure • vocabulary is ==beginning to develop== and is used with some precision
Band 4	**6–7 marks** • sentence structure is ==varied== to achieve particular effects • control of sentence construction is ==secure== • a ==range== of punctuation is ==used== accurately • spelling, including that of irregular words, is ==secure== • control of tense and agreement is ==secure== • vocabulary is ambitious and used with precision
Band 5	**8 marks** • there is ==appropriate and effective variation== of sentence structures • virtually all sentence construction is ==controlled and accurate== • a range of punctuation is used ==confidently== and accurately • virtually all spelling, including that of complex irregular words, is correct • control of tense and agreement is ==totally secure== • a ==wide range== of appropriate, ==ambitious== vocabulary is used to create effect or convey precise meaning

Improving your Section B: Questions 1 and 2 responses

Activity 12 Self-assessment

1. Now read your original responses to Section B: Questions 1 and 2. Refer back to the mark scheme for Communication and Organisation (AO5) on pages 138–139. Decide which mark your response would be given.

Understanding the mark scheme

2. Think about how you could improve the content and organisation of your response. Consider the bullet points below:

    Organisation:

    - Did you write a plan to help you organise and sequence your ideas?
    - Have you structured your writing in a way that is suitable for its purpose?
    - Have you included an engaging opening and closing?
    - Have you linked your ideas and included paragraphs to build a convincing argument?
    - Have you paragraphed your writing effectively?

    Communication:

    - Have you included some suitable features for a letter or article? For example, the article might include a bold opening statement and the letter, an address and date.
    - Have you considered who the audience is and tailored language and tone to suit them?
    - Have you engaged the reader through interesting language, ideas and techniques?
    - Does your writing show awareness of the intended reader? For example, through pronouns, imperative verbs, facts, examples and anecdotes.

3. Now refer to the mark scheme for Vocabulary, Sentence structure, Spelling and Punctuation (AO6) on page 140. Review each sentence of your writing, and decide which mark your response would be given for this mark scheme.

4. Think about how you could improve the technical accuracy of your response. Consider the bullet points below:

    a. Have you spelled all topic-specific vocabulary correctly?

    b. Have you used a range of different punctuation types?

    c. Have you varied the length and order of your sentences?

    d. Are your sentences grammatically accurate so the meaning is clear?

    e. Have you used tenses and verb agreement correctly in your writing?

5. Rewrite your responses paying particular attention to the ones that could be corrected and improved. Check your revised answers against the mark schemes to see if they would now achieve higher marks.

Upgrade

- Before you begin, know who the exact audience of your writing is. For the question asking you to write to a newspaper, the audience would be the editor working at the newspaper, rather than the readers of the newspaper.
- Be mindful of the common errors that you make. Review your work and see if your teacher has indicated any errors, for example, comma splicing, inaccurate apostrophes or incorrect use of semi-colons.

Chapter 4: Component 2

Component 2: Progress check

Now you have looked at both of the Component 2 practice papers in detail, you can review which questions you feel confident about and where you think there are improvements to be made. Look back at the 'What you have to do' lists in the 'Preparing to practise' sections of Chapter 3 and Chapter 4. These will remind you of the skills you need to demonstrate in each question.

Then, complete the following progress check.

	I am confident in this skill	I have some confidence in this skill	I need more practice in this skill
Section A			
Question 1			
I can find details in a text.			
Question 2			
I can work out how a text makes something sound appealing.			
I can select relevant evidence to support the points I wish to make.			
I can analyse the language, tone and structure in a text and how it is effective.			
I constantly refer to the question to make sure I remain on task.			
Question 3			
I can read a 19th-century text carefully, looking for specific details.			
Question 4			
I can give a clear opinion when I am being asked for my views.			
I can include a range of evidence in relation to the question to support my ideas.			
I can analyse the evidence I have selected and link this to the task.			
I can refer to the question and follow the bullet points and advice that I am given.			
Question 5			
I understand what it means to synthesise.			
I can read a text and try to pick out the overview details.			
I can explain briefly using my own words.			
I check the amount of marks on offer when answering a question.			
Question 6			
I understand what is meant by 'compare' and can compare writers' ideas from two different texts.			
I am able to read two texts and pull out the similarities and differences.			
I can support my ideas with evidence from the text.			
I understand what is meant by 'how the writers get across their feelings'.			

Component 2: Progress check

	I am confident in this skill	I have some confidence in this skill	I need more practice in this skill
Section B			
Question 1 and 2			
I understand that I have to complete *both* writing tasks in this paper.			
I understand the suggested timings for my writing.			
I understand the types of format I may be asked to use in the examination.			
I am able to work out the audience for my writing and try to appeal to them.			
I can work out the purpose of my writing.			
I can adapt my tone and style to the task set.			
I can develop detail convincingly.			
I can use carefully chosen vocabulary.			
I can use linguistic devices to enhance my writing.			
I can structure and organise my writing effectively.			
I can spell accurately.			
I can use punctuation accurately.			
I can use grammar accurately.			
I can vary my sentences effectively.			
I can use accurate and consistent tenses in my writing.			

Key terms glossary

anecdote: an amusing or interesting story about a real incident or person

aside: a remark that is intended to be heard or noticed by the reader

atmosphere: the feeling or mood of a particular place or situation

chronologically: in the order in which things occurred

cohesion: the quality of being logical and consistent

context: the words or ideas surrounding something, which can help to clarify the meaning

dialogue: the words spoken by people in a piece of writing

evaluate: to form an opinion after thinking about something carefully

explicit: stated clearly and openly

first person: when we use 'I' or 'we' as the narrative voice in a text

generalised: making a general statement and not looking at the details

imperative verb: a verb that gives an instruction

implicit: suggested but not directly expressed

indicative content: examples of content that examiners will refer to and you may draw upon as part of a successful answer

inference: something that you can find out indirectly from what you already know

linguistic devices: words or phrases that convey meaning which is different to the literal meaning of the words

metaphor: when a thing or person is described as something else for dramatic effect e.g. 'the market was a hive of activity'

narrative: a description of events or story

omniscient narrator: an 'all-knowing' narrator; a narrator who knows the story's events and character's motives and unspoken thoughts

parenthesis: an additional word, phrase or sentence inserted into a passage that is grammatically complete without it, marked off by brackets, dashes or commas

perspective: a particular attitude towards something or way of regarding something; a point of view

present tense: a tense which expresses a current activity or action

register: the level of formality used in writing or the language used by a particular group of people

retrieve: to find or extract

rhetorical question: a question that does not need an answer; used to trigger a thought

sentence structure: the way in which the words within a sentence (or sentences) are organised

simile: a figure of speech in which one thing is compared to another using the words 'as' or 'like'

specific: detailed and exact, precise

structure: the way the text is organised, how it is put together; for example, the writer may use paragraphs, different sentence types and devices such as dialogue deliberately to influence a reader

style: the way that something is written or presented

synonym: a word that means the same as another word

synthesise: to link and put together

tenses: the form of verbs used to show the time of the action, in the past, present or future

tension: a feeling of nervousness, excitement or fear when reading a text

tone: manner of expression that shows the writer's attitude, e.g. humorous, sarcastic

track: read or follow carefully the progress of the text as it develops

unabridged quotation: evidence that is not shortened to focus on what is specifically needed

unbiased: fair and does not support or favour a particular group